I0409796

Imprisoned
Without due process
My internment at Manzanar
By
Tadashi Kishi

CreateSpace

Imprisoned without due process

Cover page picture, watchtower on cover page is from Back Cover, freehand drawing by author with haiku added.
ISBN 978-1541278950
1. Japanese American – Denial of Constitutional rights
2. Relocation and internment at Manzanar, CA

Imprisoned without due process

Table of Content

Imprisoned without due process

Prologue

Throughout all seasons
Hear the voices from the past
From this humble pen

The house I lived in

People lived here once
long ago
Lights were on
and voices heard
People scurry
here and there
I was there
long ago

Look upon that house
once more
No lights are on
no voices heard
Only shadows there
that tells the past
The rooms
dare I enter?

A pen will be
my guiding light
Shine the light
into those dark corners
Live with me
the past so dear

Imprisoned without due process

Reveal the truth
that lay dormant there

Tell not simply
what I see
Shine the light
for in vivid colors
the pen will show
what's hidden there
Let the heart beat
pulse once more

Imprisoned without due process

Reach into the past
A Pen will show you the way
Find the heartbeat there

Why I write

Sometime ago, my daughter-in-law, Melanie and my son, Greg asked Yo and me if we would write about our past. Off and on, I tried to write or use a recorder but to no avail. Deep in my mind, I had to cross a bridge that spanned over a deep gorge. I was afraid to take the first step, for emotions welled up. I envisioned below on the sharp rocks: Freedom, Liberty, and Justice for all – these and all of the words in the Constitution – dashed to smithereens and washed in the blood of patriots who believe in our America, the land of the free. There is always an eerie hollow voice echoing through the gorge in my mind: "I, Franklin Delano Roosevelt, do solemnly swear … preserve, protect and defend the Constitution of the United States."

I was afraid because some of events were too painful to think about, and my heart was torn. At times tears would form or my voice would fail. Then, one day, my granddaughter Isabel asked me to write about my thoughts about my incarceration at Manzanar during World War II. It was for her class report. It is a story that remained deep and something that most *Nisei*, second generation Japanese, never spoke about that terrible experience.

My granddaughter, Isabel is an adopted child. My son Greg and daughter-in-law, Melanie had a hard time conceiving, but they still wanted to share their love with children. Finally, they decided to adopt. One day, when they were visiting us, I spent the day entertaining Isabel to make her feel at home and that she was part of the family. I remember when I was a child visiting my aunt and uncle with my parents, my aunt said, *"Maa, hontoni okiku natta ne"* (My goodness, how big you have grown). After that, they said nothing more. I stood mute by my parents all through the visit. That would never be the case with my grandchildren. On their visit, Isabel and I read books together, played hide-and-seek, said silly things, and we were having a grand time together.

Suddenly she stopped and looked at me with her blue eyes sparkling and smiling and said, "I am so happy."

Grandpa's heart melted.

On their flight home, the parents asked Isabel, "Did you have a good time?"

She answered, "Yes."

"Why do you look so sad?" they asked her.

"I miss Grandpa."

So you can see that I could not disappoint my granddaughter by not responding.

My response was not so much about the details of Manzanar and the life there but more what I had gained from that moment on - the family, grandchildren, especially Isabel, and the good people who had become a part of my life; none of this could have happened without my having gone through that terrible time in camp

After I sent the letter to Isabel, I sent another letter about things that I had not said in the first letter. I called it "Things Unsaid." It was stiff and factual like a software manual. After writing the document, I always wondered, "Will anyone bother to turn to the next page and read?" Then one day, I saw an announcement of a writing class on "Writing from Life Experience" sponsored by the Livermore Park District and taught by *Sensei,* teacher Linda Tacy. The class was scheduled for an hour and a half each week for six weeks. I have been taking the class for over three years. I am still learning.

It has been difficult to start because the story has been buried deep inside my psyche. By writing, I have begun to learn things that never I would have realized had I not started to write. It is a story of *Nisei* growing up during the Great Depression who finds he is living in two worlds. Sometimes these two worlds are at odds with each other. Threading through this story is *Okaasan*: She is the glue that holds the family together. She bears, nurtures, and dotes on her offspring. She holds fast to her culture, for there is no other recourse for her. She resists the demise of a culture.

For each writings, I have written a haiku that embodies what follows.

I have written a poem "Penned" that was a result of a class exercise to take a word or phrase from an article and write something. I took "At the news on the radio …" to correspond to the news I heard on the radio, at my Father's nursery on Sunday December 7 of the attack on Pearl Harbor. It is the pen that began to heal the torn heart.

I have learned and experienced a great deal since that time I left Manzanar to teach Conversational Japanese to US Army Reservists at the University of Minnesota. I needed to revisit Ringo-en and add to the story. First, as I looked back at barb wires, the watchtower with the searchlight, a machine gun pointed inwards at the camp ground, and a US soldier ready to fire a devastating blow on any internee that dared to cross the barb wire fencing. It was an uneasy picture.

I was the only one leaving that day on the bus and I silently asked myself, "Will something good come out of that place of imprisonment and injustice?"

I am no longer in doubt.

It was Dr. Gordon Sato who wanted something good to come out of that place of injustice. He saved a nation, Eritrea, AF from poverty to become self sufficient by using his own resources and not US Foreign Aid.

Then there was Joseph Kurihara, a veteran of WWI who stood up for his rights as an American, He is someone to behold and be rightfully proud of his Nikkei spirit.

Sadao Munemori is not the last of the 100/442 Battalion who served in Europe during WWII who served meritoriously. He is the recipient of our Nation's highest recognition of bravery and self sacrifice, Congressional Medal of Honor.

Each came out of that place of injustice. Each was honor bound.

Penned

Without telling anyone,
Going out before dawn,
Working all day by ourselves,
Shaking our heads in silence
At the news on the radio*.

What happen to you?
After the news, "The Day of Infamy," on the radio.
You open your mouth,
And there is just a gurgle.
Your mind is racing to spew its data.
From one corner of your cranium,
Screams out a voice, "I want to be heard!"
Another and another reach out,
"No, listen, I want you to know."
There is chaos in your mind
For time and space have no meaning.
Yet, from your lips a word, a sentence, may flow.
But the acid in your stomach eats away,
You feel your heart beat pulsing erratically.
A tear may drop for a voice screams,
"Remember how deep the hurt remains."
There are words but your voice is cracking.
You realize you are not making sense.
Silence is now your safe place.

Another time a granddaughter's voice is heard,
"Please tell how you felt about that time?"
You try your voice on a recorder
But that won't do.
You pick up a pen and begin to write.
The voices suppressed so long
All cry out wanting to be heard.
But your hand is now in control.

Imprisoned without due process

You will choose your moment in time.
No acid can engulf the words you write.
Your heart beats strong and sometimes wildly.
You are in control and you write
A story that long remained so deep.
"The pen is mightier that a sword," they say.
But it is more than that.
It is a brush that can paint the story,
Give life to the feelings and hope that remained so deep.
It is more than sword and paintbrush too.
It is a light that reveals what's hidden.
It is an antidote that heals the wounds.

Lines from the poem: Telephone Repairman by Joe Miller

Imprisoned without due process

The U.S. Navy took this photo of the *U.S.S. Arizona* following the Japanese attack on Pearl Harbor on December 7, 1941

CREDIT: Official U.S. Navy photograph. "*USS Arizona, at Height of Fire, Following Japanese Aerial Attack on Pearl Harbor, Hawaii.*" December 7, 1941
Prints and Photographs Division,
Library of Congress.

In 1948, I was an American GI who had just landed at Hickam Field, Oahu, Hawaii. As I stepped down on the tarmac, I was moved with deep emotion about the brave men who had answered the call to defend out great nation. To them I penned this poem.

Imprisoned without due process

Red rays from the East
Strike our Pacific fortress
Future stained in blood

"The Day of Infamy"

At the ancient shrine, Ise
A young man passes through the *Torii*
He walks with the spirits to the *Jingu*, Shrine
Silently he bows his head twice
His heart looks for *Amaterasu*, Sun Goddess
Twice he claps his hands and bows
Asks for divine guidance
Not for bountiful gifts
But loyalty to his *Bushido* spirit

To the East
Statesmen huddle around tables
Pontificate lofty ideals of peace
Each guard their secrets
Cloud of war disturbs the great white leader
A wish unsaid by the other
Silent words do not mix
Cauldron boils secretly in the seas
Suddenly the gates of Hell burst open

Aloha from Paradise
Brush cobwebs from your eyes
'Tis early Sunday morn
Pray to God and cleanse your soul
Take your weekend pass and loll around
There's no need to worry
Oahu strongest fortress in the world
Bright red sunrays strike my door

Imprisoned without due process

Hawaii's fate was sealed
The war in Europe was our priority
Move the ships and help the Brits
Our eyes are constant
The enemy was too far
Why then the blip from the north
Just our planes returning home
Bombs away, warships belly up
Red sea tainted with diesel oil

In another place
A gold star glistens in the window
Tears fall to a mother's breast
A heart was torn asunder
I raised the child to be a man
He chose the Flag his guiding light
Defend our shores from those who dare
Stood tall with brave young men
He was home a hero

Imprisoned without due process

War clouds to the East
Tsunami engulfed our lives
Dashed against barb wires

On the radio

The year was1940, President Franklin Roosevelt signed the Selective Training and Service Act, creating the first peacetime draft.

"Greetings from your Selective Service: Register for Selective Service at your local Draft Office since you are now eighteen. Your classification is 1A. Please wait for your Draft lottery numbers."

My brother's number was selected for the draft lottery and, shortly afterwards, he was shipped out to Fort Ord, Monterey, California. I lucked out, and I chided him and said, "If you're going to win a lottery, this isn't the one to win!"

While there was a growing turmoil in Europe, our country had turned to isolationism following the costly involvement of the World War I. Congress passed a series of Neutrality Acts but imposed embargos while, at the same time, permitted the sale of materials and supplies to belligerent nations.

Frank was among the thousands of young Americans drafted but it did not appear that the United States was ready to be involved in the European conflict. The US Army was still varying of Japanese Americans in the military for he said that while at Fort Ord, he was assigned drive an ambulance. Then, I was shocked and puzzled to hear from Frank that the Nisei soldiers stationed there were rounded up and held in a warehouse when the President's wife, Mrs. Eleanor Roosevelt visited Fort Ord.

"But you're a citizen, drafted and in uniform. What in the world is going on?" I asked him.

He just shook his head and nothing more was said.

While I missed seeing my brother after his visit home on his furlough, I was too busy attending UCLA to keep track of his deployment after his basic training. It was several years later that I would see him again.

It was eleven o'clock Sunday, December 7, 1941 our world collapsed.

"Come quick! Listen to what's on the radio," said my sister-in-law frantically.

Oh my God! Did you hear over the radio? Japan attacked Pearl Harbor this morning!

Our Jaws dropped and our eyes open wide in disbelief of what had happened. All we could say was, *"Why? Why? Why did this happen?"*

Mother was at home while the rest of us were working at our family nursery in Santa Monica. We were stunned as the blood drained from our faces, and a disquieting silence fell. Little did we know that a *tsunami* would sweep over our lives very soon.

It was as if everything was preplanned when the FBI, in their black sedan, screech to a halt in front of the Nursery, seized *Otoosan,* father, who was working outside in the nursery, handcuffed him, and hauled him into their car. I rushed home worried about *Okaasan*, mother while Joe and my sister-in-law tended to the nursery.

Our nightmare was just beginning on that "Day of Infamy!" When I returned home, two agents ransacked the house looking for something or anything. They questioned *Otoosan*, father mercilessly, turned our house inside out, and left everything strewn on the floor. I saw *Okaasan*'s ashen face as we all stood by horrified by what was taking place. We watched but were unable to intervene, as agents acted like Gestapo. With smirks on their faces, they questioned *Otoosan* over and over using information they had gained months before by secretly wiretapping the phones lines.

This was no happenstance, for this same scene was taking place throughout the West Coast, a well-timed effort to round up and arresting every prominent member or leaders of the Japanese community.

Imprisoned without due process

Hate had raised its ugly head and the Press, guardian of truth began publishing lies that farmers tilled their land to point at military installations and airports; Japanese fishermen were Japanese sailors in disguise monitoring naval ships and passing information to Japan; the Japanese schools were training children to be Japanese soldiers who were ready to strike at America. It brought out the worst of our country; the vermin, including the "Sons and Daughters of the Golden West, who wanted to rid the "Yellow Peril" from California. Even clergymen spewed the vitriol at Japanese.

I remember vividly the panic we felt afterwards and tragic action we took to rid ourselves of everything Japanese. We threw everything into that bonfire: books, Japanese textbooks that I had studied so diligently, photographs by the armful that we had no time to sort out, Japanese sport fencing gear, papers, drawings, and list goes on. The fire reached hungrily for everything. I saw a photograph of smiling children begin to curl away from the heat. The faces turned grotesque and I heard a silent cry, "Why me? Why me?" Suddenly it burst into flames. Finally, there was a glow of burning embers consuming the last of our family's past. Only ashes remained. Yet, those watching the tragedy were still Japanese.

It was a disquieting feeling not knowing what was happening to my father... After a few days, we were allowed to see *Otoosan* at the Tujunga Canyon Compound jailed with other *Issei*. I watched a confused and expressionless face of my father. No charges, just that he was Japanese. Ever after that day, we never knew where he was until he was finally incarcerated at the Santa Fe Federal Prison, Santa Fe, New Mexico as a POW. Then came our turn: curfew. A series of Federal Orders were issued that restricted the movement of people of Japanese ancestry from various Western Defense Zones designated by the War Department. A most famous quote by General DeWitt revealed the sentiment of many prominent people: "A dead Jap is a good Jap."

Imprisoned without due process

After two years struggling to complete the basic college requirements at UCLA, I never thought a dark shadow would cast over dreams of tomorrow, and tomorrow.

I returned to school to prepare for the end of the semester, but I moved like a mindless robot. I was apprehensive at first about what the situation would be when I returned to class, but nobody looked at me as the enemy. What I saw was worried faces among my classmates about being drafted early. A few even talked about volunteering to serve.

I had to concentrate on my class subjects because December is the month for finals before the Christmas Holidays. It's a grueling time filled anxiety about what the Professor would spring on you in the final exams. I went over and over the subjects and notes until I decided "What the heck, I can't cram any more into my head."

At last, the finals were over, and I decided to help at the nursery. I loaded up a wheelbarrow full of plants from the back of the nursery and started hauling them to the front. Suddenly the wheelbarrow slipped out of my hand as I blanked out. When my brother Joe heard the wheelbarrow drop, he came rushing out. He saw me on the ground and asked, "You ok?"

I mumbled something and got up.

"Hey, why don't you take it easy today?" he said to me.

I must have been too exhausted from cramming for the finals.

If we had been uncertain about our future, we saw it more clearly when the vermin's sprung out of their dark holes and began spewing their lies and hatred at all Japanese. The free press," guardians of truth," printed the same lies and characterized all Japanese as uncivilized beasts. Meanwhile, the President, Congress, and the Secretary of Navy were ready to act against all Japanese.

If I had been more cognizant that the world I lived in wasn't what it had seemed, I would not have been so shocked about what was happening. But I remembered what I had learned in my Samohi Civics class. After reading the Constitution, we memorized important names and dates, but never had any extensive discussion about the subject. However, the words of Patrick Henry still rings in my ears "… give me liberty or give me death!" I was always awed by those words and by our elected representative whose responsibility it was to preserve our freedom by upholding our Constitution. I can't recall the teacher ever talking about discrimination.

I remember one night, I rushed outside when I heard the sound of ack-ack and saw searchlights crisscrossing and scanning the sky while illuminating puffy clouds here and there. I looked intently, but I neither saw nor heard any airplane droning high above. It went on for several hours, but no enemy planes fell. Only a weather balloon scared the Army anti-aircraft into action.

On February 19, 1942, President Roosevelt signed Executive Order 9066. Then, on February 24, 1942, all of the West Coast was declared a "strategic area" and 9 p.m. curfew was imposed. I had to drop out of UCLA since the curfew restricted me from traveling to school, especially at nighttime to utilize the library. That was the end of my dreams of tomorrow, and tomorrow.

Then the order for evacuation came. Hatred had begun the battle cry and Governors of states where internment camps were to be constructed protested, "Not in my backyard." Forgotten are those words, "I … do solemnly swear to uphold the Constitution. …

But that was to be the least of my worries.

Imprisoned without due process

Executive Order No. 9066

The President

Authorizing the Secretary of War to Prescribe Military Areas

Whereas the successful prosecution of the war requires every possible protection against espionage and against sabotage to national-defense material, national-defense premises, and national-defense utilities as defined in Section 4, Act of April 20, 1918, 40 Stat. 533, as amended by the Act of November 30, 1940, 54 Stat. 1220, and the Act of August 21, 1941, 55 Stat. 655 (U.S.C., Title 50, Sec. 104);

Now, therefore, by virtue of the authority vested in me as President of the United States, and Commander in Chief of the Army and Navy, I hereby authorize and direct the Secretary of War, and the Military Commanders whom he may from time to time designate, whenever he or any designated Commander deems such action necessary or desirable, to prescribe military areas in such places and of such extent as he or the appropriate Military Commander may determine, from which any or all persons may be excluded, and with respect to which, the right of any person to enter, remain in, or leave shall be subject to whatever restrictions the Secretary of War or the appropriate Military Commander may impose in his discretion. The Secretary of War is hereby authorized to provide for residents of any such area who are excluded there from, such transportation, food, shelter, and other accommodations as may be necessary, in the judgment of the Secretary of War or the said Military Commander, and until other arrangements are made, to accomplish the purpose of this order. The designation of military areas in any region or locality shall supersede designations of prohibited and restricted areas by the Attorney General under the Proclamations of December 7 and 8, 1941, and shall supersede the responsibility and authority of the Attorney General under the said Proclamations in respect of such prohibited and restricted areas.

I hereby further authorize and direct the Secretary of War and the said Military Commanders to take such other steps as he or the appropriate Military Commander may deem advisable to enforce compliance with the restrictions applicable to each Military area hereinabove authorized to be designated, including the use of Federal troops and other Federal Agencies, with authority to accept assistance of state and local agencies.

I hereby further authorize and direct all Executive Departments, independent establishments and other Federal Agencies, to assist the Secretary of War or the said Military Commanders in carrying out this Executive Order, including the furnishing of medical aid, hospitalization, food, clothing, transportation, use of land, shelter, and other supplies, equipment, utilities, facilities, and services.

This order shall not be construed as modifying or limiting in any way the authority heretofore granted under Executive Order No. 8972, dated December 12, 1941, nor shall it be construed as limiting or modifying the duty and responsibility of the Federal Bureau of Investigation, with respect to the investigation of alleged acts of sabotage or the duty and responsibility of the Attorney General and the Department of Justice under the Proclamations of December 7 and 8, 1941, prescribing regulations for the conduct and control of alien enemies, except as such duty and responsibility is superseded by the designation of military areas hereunder.

Franklin D. Roosevelt
The White House,
February 19, 1942. F.R. Doc. 42–1563

Imprisoned without due process

Liberty bell rings
Born a Citizen now void
Crisis of the heart

Executive Order 9066

On February 19, 1942, President D. Roosevelt signed Executive Order 9066, authorizing the War Department to exclude any and all persons of Japanese ancestry from prescribed military areas. All people of Japanese ancestry were removed from the Western coastal regions and deported to guarded camps called "relocation camps."

When the Executive Order was announced, the War Department issued evacuation orders to Japanese families in strategic defense areas. Some families were given only forty-eight hours to move from their homes. The bigots, opportunists, vultures, and hate mongers descended on these hapless families and offered to buy their family belongings for pennies on the dollar or just take them away for nothing. We were more fortunate than they were, but to say fortunate is obscene here. Families in our area had several weeks before we would be evacuated from our homes. Several locations were designated to allow families to store items. Of course, there was no guarantee that the items would be safe from robbery, nor was there any hope that families would be able to retrieve them. Yet this storage option was the best we could hope for.

With father incarcerated, and Frank already in the U.S. Army, my brother Joe shouldered the task of taking care of the families, arranging for someone to take over the nursery, and deciding on what to keep, store, or discard. I had the responsibility of constructing wooden boxes to store some of the family belongings for storage. Mother and my younger sister, Kaz were busy sorting out the items. What to save and what to discard was no easy decision to make since storage space was limited. Except for the automobiles, we made no attempt to sell off any of the family excess belongings. My brother Joe offered other Japanese families the use of his Nursery truck and our backbreaking service to help haul any storage items free of charge.

Finally, on April 21, 1942, the day of assembly for evacuation was announced. My brother and I transported not only our baggage, but also helped others with their family belongings. At the assembly site, Santa Monica Methodist Church, several old Greyhound buses were parked and waiting for us to board. Young soldiers armed with M1s and bayonets fixed ready for action watched the commotion very closely. Families tried to stay together, but youngsters tended to ride with each other. With all of the confusion, there was no time to cry. Silently we boarded the buses, the door banged closed and we were off to some far off desolate internment camp.

I recalled other times when I rode with schoolmates when we chattered and sang "Row, Row Your Boat" and "Ole McDonald Had a Farm" so loudly that the driver could hardly keep his sanity. This was a somber ride. We might as well have been draped in black and headed to a funeral. The riders looked this way and that while showing no emotion. Tears flowing? Nonsense! We were fresh out of tears. Our bus was headed towards the Mohave dessert on US 395.

As soon as we were out of Los Angeles City, the bus driver stopped, handed each of us a box lunch, and quickly started back on the road again. It was a gourmet lunch, consisting of one bologna sandwich, an apple, and a small milk carton. No one really had the appetite to enjoy the Government's delicious meal. As the scenery passed by, my mind was too clouded with gloom to enjoy the beauty of the desert. As we approached Owens Valley, I recalled that there was once a beautiful lake here but that Los Angeles County had usurped the water rights and dried up most of the lake. To the northeast was the Panamint Range bordering Death Valley, and just west of the highway was the Alabama Hills where many Hollywood Western movies were made. I could almost picture Roy Rodgers riding Trigger here. Shortly, we arrived at a small country town among some scrubby trees. It was Lone Pine.

Imprisoned without due process

This is the place where the horror and humiliation of my life happened which I have never overcome. The driver had stopped for fuel and said he would be here for at least a half an hour or more. He pointed to the restrooms behind the station. I joined the others in a single line and waited my turn. The Men's restroom was a weather worn faded green structure, and the door seemed to just sag onto its hinges. The door was never closed during this procession. When my turn came, the scene was enough to make my stomach churn. The room was not just dusty, but dirty and unkempt. The basin was dirty with grease marks and rust stains. The faucet was green with age, and dirty water spots on the walls and floor signaled no paper towels here. Even a spider had abandoned a web that was in disarray with dust all over it. The toilet, ugh! Was it American-Standard? What every make it was, the porcelain had yellowed with age and had rusted marks dripping down the interior. What joy; it was my turn. It was a long wait, but I stood frozen before the toilet. Try as I might, nothing happened. It wasn't just the stench that overpowered me, but the mental pressure from seeing the line of males waiting their turn. I was mortified and humiliated. I muttered something inaudible, buttoned up, and walk away from the crowd. From that day on, public restrooms have been the bane of my life. The driver motioned us to return and board the bus. I often wondered why the driver had bothered to stop at Lone Pine since Manzanar was only seven miles further. We were now at the entrance of Manzanar, a guard gate manned by US Military Police. The site was surrounded with barbed-wire fence and watchtowers "for our protection," except that the searchlights and machine guns were pointed inward. The sun was just sinking behind Mt. Williamson towering high in the Sierra Nevada Range. As soon as the MP's cleared us, the bus proceeded to a place for processing. There were a number of internees waiting for us to disembark. A dust storm must have just subsided because I could see dust on the internees' clothes and faces except for the clear area around their eyes where they had removed the goggles. This was our new home, a desolate and foreboding land.

Imprisoned without due process

Manzanar Entrance

"Library of Congress, Prints and Photographs Division, LC-A35-4M-10."

Watchtower with searchlight, guard, machine gun

Imprisoned without due process

Home, in the Land of the Free

After we unloaded our belongings, we lined up and received salt tablets that we gulped down with water spooned from a 50-gallon garbage can. They said it was to replenish the salt we might have lost from the hot weather. Next, we received our processing directions and our family was assigned to our humble abode designated by K442,our family number. We picked up our belongings and trudged to our designated barrack. It was a long tar-papered building with batten boards hammered onto the tarpaper to hold them in place. There were tears and gaps here and there showing that they were slap to construction. There were six units per barrack, sixteen by twenty feet, with a bare bulb hanging from the ceiling, an oil stove, a floor made of rough green lumber that dried and exposed the ground beneath, and six metal beds (cots). Even the way of Japanese, *shikataganai* (can't be helped) or even *Gaman* (endure it), the situation was hard to swallow. No tears shed and no words of horror were uttered, just muted silence.

But wait; there was a mix up in our assignment. There were six of us according to our family designation but another family also shared the room. Finally, the paper shufflers realized their error and assigned us to barracks in a block that had been just constructed. Before settling in, our next duty on the list was preparing our bed by stuffing straw into a canvas bag for our mattress. The event was new, humiliating, and humorous experience all in one package. We were so eager to stuff the canvas bag that we forgot we had to sleep on top of this mountain of straw. I know that none of us slept that night.

The trip and the time for processing, registering, and quarter assignments had taken so long that we were too late for dinner that first day. We all waited for morning for our first meal in camp. As I watched the internees enter the mess hall on my first day for breakfast, I saw them move with somber expressionless faces like zombies marching across the serving line. Even mother had a somber look about her. If there were tears, they were dry. Mother had endured more hardship and humiliation than the rest of the family. But she had an air of stoicism, a product of cultural heritage, "*Gaman*." Around the mess hall, the only noise I heard was the "slop, slop" of the food being spooned onto the plate or, somewhere in this large room, a young child crying or fussing. As best I can recall, the first breakfast consisted of a lumpy mound of oatmeal and burnt toast. With real butter rationed, apple butter was the choice of the management. No sugar was available to the internees since most of this ration went to the "*hakugin*" managers' (Caucasian administrators) dining room. The dinner special was a shock for even the bravest and daring. The tasty entrée was a reconstituted mummified beef liver. I definitely heard a clunk when the tissue mass hit the plate. One bite was enough for me! Later, I heard that some of the food consignment set to Manzanar had stenciled on the package "Not for human consumption." I believe it!

Since our family was always isolated from a community of Japanese families, living among a camp full of Japanese and rubbing elbows day after day was a strange and new experience for me. Moreover, we were housed in a block full of strangers. Even though we were all in the same predicament, there was not even a sign of acknowledging one's presence from anyone. It was as if everyone's mouth was sewn tightly shut. While historians claim that we are essentially a homogeneous ethnic society, I was surprised to hear when my Mother said to my younger sister and me "Don't associate or become too close to the Terminal Island Japanese because they are very rough people. And don't mingle with the Boyle Heights people because some of them belong to gangs." The scuttlebutt that was floating about in camp about these two Japanese groups can be attributed to the following: The Japanese who came from Terminal Island were mainly engaged in commercial fishing. It is true that the language spoken by fishermen is very course, if not crude, by any standard. It's not too hard to understand because, in the frenzy of landing the catch, you don't say, "Please hand me the gaff!" It's all about action now and politeness be dammed. As for those from Boyle Heights, the community had become predominantly Hispanic residents with a few percentages of other races, such as, Japanese, Jewish, German, etc. During the 1930s' the young Hispanics were noted for their dress code as "Zoot-suiters." The other young people of that area, including the Japanese, had been influenced heavily by the Zoot-suiters dress and tastes.

My sister and I had no reason to co-mingle with them, but to my surprise, I found out later that, while I was in Minnesota, my sister married a young man from Terminal Island in camp! Actually, he hadn't been a fisherman. His family ran a small grocery store in that community.

I'm embarrassed to admit that Mother was also wrong on her second warning. In our block, there was a young man who had a duck tail hairdo, a mustache, and peg legged pants. All that was missing was a long chain hanging from his belt. He was indeed a zoot-suiter from Boyle Heights. He was probably one of the nicest guys I have had the pleasure of meeting. On Saturday nights, he shared his stereo system, his records, and introduced and taught social dancing, including jitterbug, to the young people in the block. Before the days of internment, my parents had had a negative view about American style dancing. The descriptive words they used were "*Shiri furi dansu!*" This is roughly translated as "Fanny shaking dance!" For all of the fanny shaking we did, we had many enjoyable Saturday nights that probably preserved our sanity and made camp life more bearable.

How could there be any culture clash in the camp? After all, we had burned or destroyed everything Japanese in order to shed our Japanese identity when the war with Japan broke out. Most of us had either lost our worldly possessions or stored them somewhere with the small hope of recovering them at some unknown future date. What we carried was what we were. But, no matter what we did, we were still Japanese. All of those cultural values that our parents had passed on to us through our daily lives remained; *gaman* (endure), *gambaru* (persevere), *giri* (duty), *oyakoko* (loyalty), *on* (filial piety), and *kodomo no tame ni* (sacrifice for the children).

At first, family members joined each other at mealtime but this in time became a meaningless exercise. However, family life in camp was no longer what it was before the internment. Mealtime that gave us a sense of togetherness and family structure had become a community affair. The home that gave us privacy and security was an open book. No longer was there a sense of pride, self-respect, or dignity in our life of confinement. Our daily life was monotonous, haphazard, and self-defeating motions just to fill the time that had no ending. It was truly a state of mind of hopelessness (*shikata ga nai*). How could we reconcile our predicament? How could we find solace or support from the family when explicit feelings were never expressed in Japanese family? No, there were no cultural clashes per se within the family that I can recall during my brief stay in camp. But a storm was brewing among the internees.

Imprisoned without due process

Manzanar Street scene

Manzanar Street scene and Winter scene

"Library of Congress, Prints and Photographs Division, LC-A35-4-M-10."

Imprisoned without due process

Culture turned to dust
What was is no longer here
It met its demise

Demise of a culture

With one stroke of the pen, my parents' culture was left in shambles. *Issei* fathers, who were the breadwinners and authority figures of the family, were no longer relevant in the Internment Camp. Prior to the internment, prominent members of the Japanese community established Japanese schools and recreational facilities for their children in order to teach them the language and their culture. Other *Issei's* donated from their meager income to help support the schools. But successful businessmen and prominent members of the Japanese Community were quickly rounded up after December 7 and incarcerated in Federal Prisons as "Prisoners of War." Their whereabouts were often unknown. *Issei's* who are interned at Manzanar, were barred from participating in the local governing affairs. Day after day, I saw them sitting on their doorsteps dejected, rejected, and disbelieving what had happened to their lives and fortunes in America. I wondered often, "What are they thinking? Will they rise above their silence?"

English only was strictly enforced within the camp discussions. Teaching Japanese within the camp was disallowed for fear of infusing nationalism into the children. But the Japanese language is difficult and complex. How else would I, a *Nisei* understand my heritage? How else would I communicate intelligently with my *Issei* parents? The Japanese schools were looked at as hotbed for subversive teachings. I found nothing of the sort. I attended Japanese school after attending public school and on Saturdays. I am grateful that I had that opportunity to learn about the heritage of my parents.

It seems worth noting that the US Government would come to depend on our knowledge of Japanese. It was the knowledge of the Japanese language that we received by attending Japanese schools that proved to be vital to our country in war with Japan. It

is ironic that prior to December 7, the US Army had set up a
Military Intelligence School at Presidio of San Francisco to train
Niseis in Military Japanese in case we had a war against Japan. My
brother, drafted before December 7, was later assigned to the
Military Intelligence School. Without diminishing the heroic action
of the *Niseis* on the European front, the *Nisei* Military Intelligence
Service (MIS) has been recognized as shortening the war in the
Pacific by more than two years. Later, I would also graduate from
MIS Presidio of Monterey, California and serve as an interpreter in
Japan during 1947 - 1948.

     Mother's role was in shambles too. We were now all wards
of the US government such that her role to nurture, dote, protect
her children become a meaningless exercise. Her children scattered
as soon daybreak came. There was nothing here that reminded us
of home. Back home our family had sat together for supper every
day. There was a set protocol: *Otoosan* served first, *chonan* (first
born son) next, and the rest in the order or their ages. But we were
family together as one. There was always the familiar scent of soy
sauce in the air. And *Ocha*, green tea instead of milk was on the
table and rice our main staple. *Okaasan* was always busy cooking
and serving. She was always last to sit down with us. The kitchen
was her domain. Even *Otoosan* rarely entered that sacred place.
Now, the family that had been was no longer present.

     Her kitchen was replaced by the mess hall. Her children sat
with their friends and sometimes ate at a different block mess hall.
I too was guilty of that indiscretion. And why not go when
someone would say, "Hey, the cook in Block 2 is serving beef
tonight instead of the usual slop in our mess hall?" Life was just
game to survive in this hellhole.

Mess Hall

Mess hall

"Library of Congress, Prints and Photographs Division, LC-A35-4-M-10."

Imprisoned without due process

From this desert bloom
Petals fall from cutting winds
Will it bloom once more?

The Room

Freedom lies in dust

A sixteen by twenty foot room
Squeezing in five or more people
Bussed to this desert terrain
It's for your own good they say
Too much hate for your safety outside
It's your patriotic duty in time of war
Silent are the words, Freedom and Liberty

Hanging blankets define my space
In this sixteen by twenty foot room
Tarpaper building gives no solace
Hastily built construction leaves a view
Desert land beneath and scorpions too
Starry skies above so cold and forbidding
Hollow are the words Justice for All

Barbwires and watchtowers your safety net
Searchlights your guiding light
For this sixteen by twenty foot room
The desert wind blows wickedly
Dust streams through the cracks
Ashen scenery has become this place
We are but one, dust

Silent faces in this room
Laughter a word unknown
Walls around me threaten to crush my will
It's only a sixteen by twenty foot room

Imprisoned without due process

No chairs to sit to catch my breath
No table to rest my disquieted mind
No open door brings freedom

Day by day this is your space
Walls have ears for they are thin
No need to lock the door, for what's to lose
You lost your home and life-long dreams
Nothing left for this sixteen by twenty foot room
Take your time and enjoy the stay
No need to think what tomorrow brings

This the wasteland that I must face
The wind does blow whirling missiles
Etching its path across my skin
Shikataganai (It's fate) looms in my face
I vow I will not die on this reservation
By living in a sixteen by twenty foot room
For freedom lies beyond the gates

What will I remember?

On the first day of school,
A little girl runs home crying
Holding the child and comforting her, mother asks,
"You were so happy to go to school in your new dress.
I saw you skipping merrily on your way.
Why are you home so early and why are you crying?"
With tears soaking her mother's breast, she sobs,
"There's nothing Mommy.
No chairs, no pictures on the wall.
There's not even a flag I used to pledge allegiance to!
Oh Mommy, Mommy let's go back to America."
Child's naked truth: This sixteen by twenty foot room

Imprisoned without due process

In the dust your shot
Typhoid Mary's legacy
Angel voice, wake up!

Waking Up

Religion was never a big thing in my life. That's because my Japanese parents were never associated with any church. While the family on special occasions followed Shinto Rites and Buddhist Ceremonies, the two are not religions, in the sense of Judeo-Christian. I did, however, attend Methodist Church's Sunday school in my youth. Later, when I was older, I became a teenage Methodist. On Sundays, I listened to the Pastor's sermon but he talked in a low monotone voice that droned on and on. If he had a message, I didn't hear it. I was never baptized. Nevertheless, Christian faith was in my blood. At Manzanar, I had a wake-up call.

I remember the first day when our bus entered Manzanar. Dust never settles here. Tired from our travel, we staggered off the bus and met fellow internees waiting to process us for our incarceration. One handed us our schedule for processing. Another handed us three salt tablets and motioned us go to an internee standing near galvanized garbage. He dipped a big metal ladle into the garbage and said, "Swallow your salt tablets and wash them down with this." He shoved the ladle full of water towards us. I was astonished. He didn't even bother to clean the ladle for each internee. Then our fellow internees motioned us to a barrack for our first typhoid shots. But it seems that I needed two shots to protect me from typhoid fever.

It was several weeks later that I had my second typhoid booster shot. It was Sunday the next day when a friend from my hometown said, "Our pastor is visiting Manzanar and will be giving a sermon. Let's go hear what he had to say."

"You mean there's a church in this camp?" I asked.

"Yeah, it's a barrack building in block 15.

Imprisoned without due process

Not much choice in what I could wear to church since all I could bring to camp was about 80lbs or what I could carry. At least I had a clean shirt and pair of slacks. I walked with my friend across the firebreak to block 15. When I entered, the room was nearly full of people, standing, for there was no furniture, only a makeshift pulpit in front.

Someone introduced the pastor and he began his sermon. I recognized him immediately. He was my soft-spoken clergyman from Santa Monica. I remember the day we assembled at his church. I saw him busily helping people who wanted to use the church facilities before boarding the bus for Manzanar. While I tried listening to his sermon, his voice didn't carry too far in the hastily built tarpaper barrack. But true to what I recall from his sermons back home, he proceeded to drone on and on. I was trying to pay attention when I noticed that my vision was changing. Darkness was gradually descending from the top of my vision downward. I tried forcing my eyes to open wider but a shade seemed to close over my eyes. Suddenly, my legs felt rubbery. I knew I was in trouble. I fought hard to stay erect but it was no use. I forced myself to gently squat down to the floor between the people around me. I was halfway down but I can't remember what happened after that.

If I was supposed to hear Angels, I don't remember. If I was at the Pearly Gate, I don't remember seeing Saint Peter. I can't remember how long I was on the floor, but when I woke up, there, staring down at me, was my Pastor.

He looked at me very concerned and asked, "Are you all right?" I was startled, if not totally embarrassed and didn't reply.

Then, someone yelled, "Move back and give him some air!"

I did not return for another awakening. But this was not the last of my enlightenment with religion. My brother Joe, his wife Yo, and his father-in-law had moved to their own lodging while, Okaasan, my younger sister, Kaz and I remained in our old room. We were all caught up in our miserable world trying to make the best of our situation. Okaasan, of course, had more than her share or worries. While I was busy with my teaching assignment, mother had, in the meantime, spent her days at the Maryknoll Catholic Church established at Manzanar. She had heard that the Catholic Father was helping wives locate their husbands who had been hauled off and imprisoned by the FBI. Since I was busy preparing for my Physics class, I had lost track of her whereabouts. But one day in our room, she told me spending her time at the Catholic Church. She said she was beholden to the Church Father and accepted the Catholic faith and was baptized. And she had encouraged my sister, Kaz to attend the Catechism classes to become a Catholic. She then asked me if I would attend the Catechism classes for her.

I was totally unprepared for her request and said that I wasn't sure that I wanted to be a Catholic. For all of the Sundays I attended the Methodist Church at Santa Monica, I never considered being baptized even though I accepted Christian moral values. Normally I would have consented to her wishes, but I told her I was sorry that I was too busy to take the Catechism classes. I thought the issue was settled, but again a few weeks later, she asked me once more. This time she was more insistent. I reluctantly relented.

I had dubious feelings as I walked across the firebreak towards the Catholic Church located in the Recreation Building in block 25. After signing in, I listen intently to the first day session. I failed the Catechism instructions. When I saw Okaasan again, I said I was sorry but I was not interested in continuing. She quietly accepted my words; the subject of religion was closed for ever.

Imprisoned without due process

Diabolic wish
Yes, Yes; No, No; I can't win
Nightmare of the Heart

Trouble in Paradise

"Hey you guys," someone yelled, "there's something big going on near the Administration building and the Manzanar police station. Come join us and see what's happening!"

It was Sunday, December 6, 1942 when a few of us were passing the time playing basketball. "Sure, why not," we called out and joined him. When we arrived at the scene, there was a crowd of people standing by looking towards the police station. Someone was shouting something, but I couldn't make out what he was saying, nor did I know why he or she gathered there. I looked over the shoulder of the spectators and saw a small group of armed soldiers facing the crowd. I was shocked to see one soldier sitting on the ground with a machine gun fully loaded – It was the exact model of machine gun (45 calibers Thompson sub-machine gun) that I had practiced with when I took ROTC at UCLA. At that moment, I knew this was not the place for me to be! The young recruits looked too trigger-happy for my money. I left the scene quickly and returned to my humble abode. It was later that day that I heard that a young *Nisei* had been shot and killed at the scene where I had been earlier. There were 11 other casualties. Most of the wounds were from the side or from the back. A second later died of his injuries. Of the 12 shot, 4 were *Niseis,* 2 were *Isseis,* and 5 were *Kibeis* (*Niseis* who were sent by their parents to Japan for education and later returned to the United States). Apparently the crowd had become unruly, and the guards responded by tossing tear gas grenades into the crowd. It was during this commotion that the soldiers panicked and fired into the crowd. How could such a terrible tragedy transpire?

There was enough guilt to go around for everybody for this terrible tragedy. The main factors that contributed to this confrontation were the degrading and hopeless camp environment and the suspicions, rivalry for control of the camp politics, and cultural differences between *Niseis*, on the one hand, and the *Isseis* and *Kibeis* on the other. Then there were the rabble-rousers who had no better things to do but to add to an explosive confrontation. The homogeneous ethnic society was no longer homogeneous.

This event began a day earlier. On December 5, 1942, violence broke out at Manzanar. The moment was ripe for conflicts between *Niseis* and *Kibeis*. A month earlier, three *Niseis*, Fred Tayama, Joe Masaoka, and Kiyoshi Higashi, active member of the JACL, received permission from the War department to represent Manzanar at a weeklong JACL convention in Salt Lake City. At the convention, they supported the resolution urging the War Department to draft *Niseis* for the American armed forces. Once again, the JACL, an organization that had never been officially selected to represent the rest of the Japanese population, was making decisions that affected all of the internees. When Fred Tayama returned to Manzanar, many evacuees considered him an informer (*Inu*) for FBI and the camp (WRA) administrators. On the night he returned, he was badly beaten up by several masked men but managed to survive. Tayama identified Harry Ueno, a *Kibei* as one of the assailants. Subsequently, Ueno was arrested and placed in jail, but not at Manzanar. Ueno, who had organized the Kitchen Workers' Union at Manzanar, was popular with the *Kibeis* and *Isseis* and with the anti-JACL crowd. He was also at odds with Tayama who had formed the JACL affiliated Manzanar Works Corps. But these two individuals were pawns of larger issues that were fomenting within the camp.

Who in his right mind could ever conceive of a diabolical set of questions based on the presumption that loyalty could be determined by a questionnaire? No other piece of paper (February 1943) could be more divisive between family members than the following two questions:

No. 27: Are you willing to serve in the armed forces of the United States on combat duty, wherever ordered?

No. 28: Will you swear unqualified allegiance to the

Imprisoned without due process

United States of America and faithfully defend the United States from any and all attack by foreign or domestic forces, and foreswear any form of allegiance or obedience to the Japanese Emperor, or any other foreign government, power, or organization?

There was a buzz in the air, for rumors were running rampant about this announcement. The word was out that the questionnaire was labeled/presented/billed as an "Application for Leave Clearance" but in reality, it was clearly a loyalty oath to draft eligible *Nisei*, second generation Japanese Americans, into military service. The memorandum stated that a $10,000 fine and/or twenty years imprisonment would be imposed if an individual refused to answer and sign the forms. The Isseis, who are non-citizens, were also required to sign off on the same questionnaire.

There was a meeting scheduled to discuss this new turn of events that had created a crisis within the camp. I was anxious to attend to find out what the Government had in store for us. When the meeting started, I felt the tension in the air. It could explode at any minute. Mostly men and young *Niseis* and *Kibeis* were there. There were no women attending this meeting. Only a handful of *Isseis* were there for they had been relegated to non-participant in the camp's affairs.

I listened intently to the speaker's every words as he read the memorandum verbatim.

Someone shouted from the side, "What the hell is this all about? They take everything from us and now they want to do what?"

"Yeah, explain," someone voiced angrily.

I turned toward the agitator and nodded my head, agreeing with his protest.

The speaker waved his hand, "Let me finish," as he said loudly.

"Answering the questionnaire is necessary in order to determine who can be allowed to leave the camp," he continued.

Imprisoned without due process

Someone stood up and said, "I don't understand." He raised his voice: "They said that Manzanar was a Relocation Center from where we could leave eastward at anytime. There was never any Loyalty Questionnaire required. This is the same bull they fed us when they said leaving the Western Defense Area was our patriotic duty."

The speaker, looked flustered, spoke up, "I'm just here to tell you about this memorandum. I have no idea what the intent is except that it was given to me as an 'Application for Leave.'"

An older man stood up. "I'm an *Issei*. When World War I broke out, I volunteered to serve because they said I could become a citizen. I was a citizen until Pearl Harbor. They took my citizenship away saying that I'm an enemy alien, unqualified as an American. Now they turn around and hand me this crap. What do my answers mean anyway? 'Yes, yes' and I'm still a Jap - doesn't make much sense."

A young man in the back rose and spoke, "How can I forswear my allegiance to the Emperor when I have never been to Japan? In fact, I don't even speak Japanese." It seems I'm guilty because my parents are Japanese. Who drafted this anyway?"

At last I stood up, found my voice and said, "I can't help but believe that the government is Hell bent on destroying the Japanese family. *Isseis* can only answer "No, no" because the Law says they cannot become citizens. So, if they answer otherwise, they become a person without a country or Persona non-Grata. For myself, the government has reclassified me 4-C, enemy alien. So am I alien or not? May I add that my father was arrested because he was a prominent member of our local Japanese Community. There was nothing sinister about his service to the Japanese Community. All he wanted to do was to provide *Niseis* the knowledge about the Japanese language and culture that defined who the *Isseis* are. We have no knowledge of his whereabouts or even whether we will ever see him again. On top of that, my brother is serving in the US Army Military Intelligence Service. I'm sure a number of you are in the same predicament. Rumor has it that "No, no's" will be sent to Tulelake, a detention camp where these individual will become pawns for prisoner exchange. If I sign "Yes, Yes" while my mother can only answer "No, No" what's left of my family will be torn apart and never see one another again. What kind of justice is that?"

My voice was cracking. Others, around me were shaking their heads and agreeing. "Yeah, there's no justice here."

Another individual stood up and said, "Why don't the *Hakujin's* (Caucasians) come down here and give us some real answers?"

The speaker waved his hands and muttered something inaudible. The meeting came to an end. Red faces angered at the confusing memorandum grumbled and headed back to their tarpapered rooms.

With a solemn face and heavy in thought, I joined the others and left. This was early February and I still had my Physics class to prepare for the following day. Outside the night was cold but clear. As I walked between the barracks, I see the rooms within the camp were dimly lit with the bare incandescent lights hanging from the ceilings. Suddenly, the searchlights swept across the camp reminding me I was not free.

Imprisoned without due process

Ringo (Apples), land is parched
Gnarled limbs, no fragrance in air
Please blossom once more

Lovely Apple Orchard, Manzanar

One afternoon, I had a chance to wander around the camp. I saw the remnants of an orchard among the tarpaper buildings. There was no fragrance in the air, no white and pink blossoms of apple trees, only gnarled limbs on trees standing in what was once row after row of fruit trees. People from this valley told stories how this valley was a thriving apple and pear growing area. But the City of Los Angeles had sucked the lifeblood out of this thriving orchard by draining water from Owens Valley for its own use. Slowly the water table dropped, and the orchard succumbed to the arid soil. Sage and Manzanita brushes gradually set roots on this desert-like soil. Rattlesnakes, scorpions, tarantulas, and other desert life took over the land. Trees here and there reached deep for nutrients, but disease and insects ravaged those that were still standing. These desert dwellers had shown resilience to the ravages of time. As I looked about, it seemed so odd and yet ironic that this was an image of my parent's plight. The life of once proud and industrious Isseis had now been sucked dry of their energy and left without hope for the future. The fruits of their labor were no longer needed. They were not allowed to impart their wisdom and help participate in governing this camp. They were left to their own devices to survive this nightmare.

To the west and above the barbed wires and watchtowers, I could see Mount Williamson reaching high into the sky. Just five miles south was Mount Whitney, California's highest peak. White streaks of snow in the shadows of the sun graced the rocky tower. To the north of Mount Williamson, there was an outline of a canyon that reached towards the west and across the Sierra range. Much of the foothills looked barren, but just southwest of the barbed wire fences, a streak of greenery snaked upward along the foothills. Dogwood and other shrubbery grew along this rivulet that fed water into the valley. As I panned the foothill further, I could see a few cottonwood trees lining both sides of a dirt road that led into the camp. The trail winds passed a grove of trees with treetops and branches dead from the lack of water. A tinge of excitement rushed over me. Someday, I thought, I must follow that road over to that stream.

In my moment of reflection of the scenery, I forgot that this was late afternoon. To the north a whirling cloud appeared. It was one of the dust storm that ravaged this valley almost every day during the hot season. They move with such ferocity they caught you unprepared. Dust, pebbles, sand, and grit engulfed you in a moment's notice. I turned my back from the wind, rolled up in a ball, and tried to hold my breath as best as I could. The back of head was peppered and my skin felt like sand paper had scrapped across it. My hair. Oh my God my hair felt as if I have been sticking my head in sand pile. I kept my eyes closed because I had forgotten to bring my goggles for this terrible reception. All I could think during that horrible moment were the stories I had read about nomads in the Sahara Desert that huddled against their camels until the sand storm subsided.

Every internee tells about the terrible dust storms at Manzanar, but none can match the experience of this man: It was one summer afternoon when the dust storm started to whip up across the valley floor, picking up everything that was loose. Suddenly the gust that was sweeping across the firebreak began to turn into a whirlwind. Its path now became unpredictable. It skirted a row of tarpaper buildings and headed directly at the block's latrine. A thunderous roar, a loud boom, a terrible shaking of the latrine, and the roof flew off and sides of the building fell away. There sitting on a toilet bowl was a man stunned, dazed, and shaken.

Imprisoned without due process

Dust storm

"Library of Congress, Prints and Photographs Division, LC-A35-4-M-10."

Imprisoned without due process

Liberty bell rings
Born a Citizen now void
Crisis of the heart

Decision

The time had come to make my decision. It was February 1943, and the US Government demanded we answer two loyalty questions, Numbers 27 and 28, or suffer the consequence of a fine of $10,000 and imprisonment.

No. 27 Are you willing to serve in the armed forces of the United States on combat duty, whenever ordered?

No. 28 Will you swear unqualified allegiance to the United States of America and faithfully defend the United States from any and all attack by foreign or domestic forces, and foreswear any form of allegiance or obedience to the Japanese Emperor, or any other foreign government, power, or organization?

No other racial group members have been required to answer these questions in order to determine their loyalty. How could anyone conceive of a divisive and unjust questionnaire for both non-citizens and citizens? My life was a nightmare and my heart was torn to shreds to answer these two questions that cut deep into our family's future. I was 21 years old, a citizen classified 1A before I was imprisoned, but without due process, reclassified by the Government as 4C, enemy alien. It seems that the reclassification was a convenient ploy to incarcerate me as an enemy alien. At no time did I have the opportunity to voice my protest, even though our Constitution guaranteed my "Rights" as citizen. Now that Government wants to draft all *Niseis,* my draft status is back to 1 A, citizen. This fact alone made my answer "Yes, Yes" and "No, No" and enigma.

At first, my mother, younger sister, and I shared a sixteen-by-twenty foot room with my brother's family and his father-in-law. Later I lived with mother and my younger sister. Our furniture was stark, a potbelly oil stove for heat and an army cot with a canvas bag mattress filled with straw for each of us. There was no privacy. At night, I could see the stars through the torn tarpapered roof. Every day, every hour, and every minute, we were now wards of the government. The winds blew and dust invaded our privacy. Every bite at mealtime tasted gritty for dust was now a part of me.

Mother, sister, and I each faced a soul-searching decision that could separate us for life. My mother's only choice was "No, No." She could be deported and might never see her family, her husband who was imprisoned elsewhere, and her son who was in the US Army. My decision would not be taken lightly for Mother's life had been shattered and had suffered enough. I would not add to her misery nor will I leave her and let her bear this nightmare alone! I would decide not for myself, but in order to stop this insanity and face the consequence. I sign "No, No."

What utter stupidity by the WRA. The Army realized that they had made a mistake in requiring all internees to sign off on the poorly worded questionnaire. But the damage was done. It had caused great consternation and dissension among the people in camp. Realizing that a mistake had been made, an alternate set of questions was written for Japanese American women and for the *Isseis,* but the powers-to-be realized this too would only lead to more uncertainties and did not push this change openly. Now that I had committed myself, what was the consequence of my action?

Imprisoned without due process

Take one step forward
I will not die on this land
*For **Hate** brought me here*

One Step Forward

If I could go back and speak to Okaasan, I would tell her many things. I would tell her that there is more to our story in camp. I know that I was so busy trying to cope with my own dilemma that I didn't pay enough attention to her plight. After a few days of settling into the routine of doing nothing in particular, I needed to find a job within the camp. When I went down to the Administration office and studied the postings, I noticed that earlier internees had taken all of the office jobs. What was left was a posting for swampers. When I went to apply at one of the warehouses, I saw several young Niseis inside the building sitting around chatting while a supervisor was busy at his desk shuffling papers. The supervisor explained that the job required someone who was strong enough to help unload merchandise delivered to the camp. He accepted my application and said I could start work that day. The job was boring since most of the time was spent waiting for orders to move merchandise. Unloading twenty tons of soap or cement can be backbreaking, but once everyone got into the rhythm of tossing these heavy items, the task would go rapidly. The work was sweaty, dusty, and everyone invariably ended up cuts and scratches that looked like they'd had a fight with a wildcat. At the end of an exhausting day, I felt that, at least another day had passed in this hellhole. But this job left something to be desired. Usually the day dragged on with nothing to do, and I often wished I could find something more productive than just sitting around waiting for the truck to come in. Then, one day, my prayer was answered. I saw a posting for applicants to train for teaching assignments under the Manzanar School Program.

On the first day, there were over 200 people interested in

the program. After hearing the requirements to teacher accreditation, the number of applicants dwindled to about sixty college-trained evacuees. The program required applicants to take University of California Extension courses in education, psychology, educational psychology, American Institutions, test and measurements, and secondary education to meet the minimum requirement for a provisional teaching credential. The extension courses were taught under the auspices of the University of California. Fortunately, there were enough qualified teachers among the school administration to teach the courses. Because the program required individual commitment to complete 24 units of educational courses, the number of applicants quickly dropped to 23. I was determined to meet the challenge.

One crisp and clear night, while I was crossing a firebreak on my way to a night class, I stopped for a moment and thought about my dilemma: teaching was challenging and a step forward, but was this all I wanted out of my life? As I looked all around me from the expansive firebreak, all I could see were the dim lights in the tarpaper buildings. I envisioned people in their one-room homes just trying to make the best out of their terrible predicament. It was an uneasy uncomforting thought. Once more I looked at this desolate place and said silently to myself, "I am not about to die on this reservation." I was angry. But once again I had to look around me. Manzanar personified Hate. Hate is what brought me here, and I vowed that "hate" would not be a part of my vocabulary. For now, I had made a commitment to teach. I had something to look forward to, something good. I was determined to do my best.

I studied the required courses diligently even though some of the subjects were boring. I completed twenty-four units of educational courses. Finally, I was approved to teach high school Physics. The school, from Kindergarten through High School, was located in Block One along with the Project's Administration offices. My office was located in a laundry room that was modified to for office and science class supplies. On the first day, I met two Niseis, Mas Nakagawa and Hideyu Uyeda who were assigned to teach Chemistry. We chatted awhile and began looking over the supplies for our classrooms. There wasn't much to see. We had to improvise to make up for the lack of basic science equipment. My classroom was at the north end of a barrack. I knew the classroom would be no better than our own family barrack, so I didn't expect much. I could feel no warmth in this room; the walls were unpainted plasterboards, the floor was dark linoleum, a table in front of the classroom served as a desk, a blackboard stood along the front wall, but it was homemade and painted black. Throughout the semester the blackboard was a challenge, a friend as well as a foe. At first, the chalk would show on the blackboard, but gradually the black paint would wear off. Finally, gaps in my writing would leave the student guessing as to what I was writing on the blackboard. Because even the required number of textbooks was missing, I spent many hours preparing for our classes and duplicating lessons on a ditto machine. This duplicating process was a nightmare: First, I had to write the information with a special ink-pencil, second I would transfer the written material onto a soft gelatin surface, push a roller over it and embed the ink into it. Next, I had to place my blank paper and push a roller over it to transfer the ink to the paper. Each sheet would become progressively dimmer. Worse still, the gelatin would begin to disintegrate into one purple mess.

This was my first day: As I looked over my students, I didn't see happy faces, only puzzled looks wondering, "Who is this teacher who can't be much older than I?" However, they showed respect for me as their teacher, because Isseis have always taught children to respect authority and, especially, a "Sensei." It is part of their culture. I was not nervous for I was focused on my responsibility: teach them Physics, a subject I was confident about. As I looked at the students while conducting the class, I could see who was earnestly seeking an education and those who were simply occupying space. The latter usually sat in the back trying not to be seen or called on to participate. There were rumors that some parents wanted Caucasian teachers even though the Niseis were more qualified in the particular subject matter.

Try as I might, camp life was not an environment where

you could motivate the students to study. Even the cultural pressure to study hard was nonexistent. I often wondered if I was too tough on the students or if the material was getting through to them. But I am no longer in doubt. It was fifty years later when I received a call from one of the students who had been in my Physics class. He wanted to visit me. He told me that after he graduated from Manzanar High School, he had received a bachelor's degree in biochemistry at USC in 1951 and a PhD in biophysics from Cal Tech in 1955. He was ready to leave for a scientific project in Eritrea. He said he had just wanted to thank me for inspiring him to get a college education. I was humbled by his words. Just one student inspired makes worthwhile all the effort of my teaching.

Our World

1943 · 1944

Manzanar High

Imprisoned without due process

Science Teachers (left to right)
Mas Nakagawa, Chemistry, Tad Kishi, Physics
Hideo Uyeda, Chemistry
Photos from:Manzanar High School 1944
 Annual (Photographer,Miyatake)

Imprisoned without due process

Hold onto your seat
Hard to see clearly right now
What a spectacle

Myopia

Learning by the seat of the pants can be disastrous. For several weeks, after preparing the lessons for my high school Physics class, I seemed to develop headaches. It didn't seem to go away.

I had always thought that my eyesight was ok. In fact, I assumed that I had inherited good genes from my parents. Father was the only one that wore glasses and that was after his cataract operation. Why should I have worried? After all, I had passed all eye tests for physical exams and for the Department of Motor Vehicles' driver license.

At the Manzanar School office bulletin, there was a notice about physical exams offered by the Manzanar Hospital. "Well, why not check about my headaches?" I thought to myself. At the hospital, a doctor examined me and said, "Everything looks fine. What you need is glasses. Let me make an appointment with the Optometrist for you."

This was my first trip to the eye clinic. The whole process went by ones and twosies. While sitting in a chair, the optometrist placed a contraption with a set of lenses in from of my face. He began with an initial lens setting and went through sequence as he changed lenses:

He asked, "Is one better than two?"

From each setting I chose as "better," he continued, "Is one better than two?"

The onesie and twosies stopped when I no longer could differentiate between the two sequences. From that point, he checked for astigmatism with the final lens setting in place and a new set of lenses to measure the distortion of the test pattern.

Imprisoned without due process

Satisfied with his examination, he said, "You are near sighted and you also have astigmatism in your left eye. Let me measure you for glasses and order you a pair."

I noticed that he was having trouble testing a sample pair glasses. First, my nose is flat because my brother, Frank, occasionally gave me a bloody nose. That was the lame excuse I told people. Second, I have no distinct bridge that will allow most glasses to seat properly.

The optometrist decided on the frame and said, "Come back in two weeks and pick up your glasses."

The day for my glasses arrived. The optometrist adjusted the frame to fit me. The whole event cost me nothing because I was a ward of the US Government. After thanking the doctor, I proceeded to walk back to my humble abode wearing my spectacles.

It was weird! For every step I took, the hallway floor, seen through my new glasses, seemed to be somewhere else. My brain was signaling my leg that the floor was further down, even though my foot had already touched the floor. I walked to the exit as if I were walking on eggshells.

Then I was faced with a shocker. I had to walk down a short set of steps. My eyes would send signals to my brain but my foot and brain was not in sync. For each step, I hung onto the railing and carefully lowered onc foot at a time until I could feel each tread of the step. For a moment I knew I would have been embarrassed if any friend saw me in that awkward moment.

Back in our sixteen-by-twenty room, we had no cabinet or shelf to place or store things. I thought the safest place was to put them in the back pocket of my one and only good clean pants until I actually needed them. A few days later, I was tossing a football with friends from my hometown. We were going to form a team to play against another group of kids. Just as we were bending over in a huddle, I suddenly felt cold air coming through the seam of my pants. Oops, the seam had given out and my underwear was showing. My friend's had a good laugh but they were kind enough to gather around me and escort me back to my room.

Imprisoned without due process

I changed to my good pants and sat down for a moment. I heard a crunch.

Oh my God! I forgot I had my glasses in the back pocket! I reached back and pulled out my squished spectacles.

Imprisoned without due process

Capture its spirit
Life's hardship of Manzanar
Build Taiko Bashi

Taiko Bashi

I began to notice in this desert land that *Issei's* began to heal their wounds by revealing what lives deep inside, the love of nature and its simplicity. I saw simple gardens, carvings from Manzanita, and most of all, a rock garden indigenous of this valley. Even apple trees blossomed. In the spring of 1943, life in the camp had returned to a more peaceful mood since that terrible period of strife and violence that had resulted in the death of young Niseis. School is in full session, and children and adults are participating in various outdoor activities. Health Services are available, religious organizations are very active, and the Project has allowed and encouraged industrial operations in the manufacturing of clothing, furniture, and farm products and created a Japanese garden within the camp grounds.

The old folks have captured the spirit of nature with the Japanese garden built among the apple orchard. A small stream meandered around through the garden. Boulders and rocks of various sizes picked from the hills nearby were placed in varying patterns. The objects were not neatly stacked nor arranged in regular fashion, for nature is the ideal and regularity is not nature's way. A large boulder sat in the stream while another hung partially over the water. Look, a bridge spanned the meandering stream that was made from branches and limbs selected from trees outside the project. Each piece seemed to be carefully selected for the structure. The bridge arched in the traditional way of the *TaikoBashi,* Drum Bridge. Flat rocks of varying sizes were nestled in the ground and placed in a curved but irregular fashion and led to the bridge. They were placed in such a way that suggested to the visitor to leisurely stroll along the path and even an invitation to pause to enjoy the wonders of nature.

Imprisoned without due process

When children saw the unique shape of the bridge, it was like a magnet drawing the youngsters to try climbing to the top. Two young girls would happily walk and skip into the garden. They would jump from one stepping rock to another until they came to the bridge. They giggled as they looked at each other and pointed to the bridge. Standing next to the foot of the bridge, they try would walk but the circular arched path is too steep. Then they could face against it and slowly reach out with one arm to hang on while they brought one foot onto the bridge, put the other hand up to grab onto any part of the bridge, and pull and try to find a spot for the other foot. They would slowly repeat this ritual until they reach the top. They would be pleased with their success as they looked around the garden from their vantage point. They would seem puzzled about going down and might decide to turn around and face the bridge and climb slowly down, foot, hand, foot, hand until to the bottom. Or they might hold and slide down on the fanny. But there is no place to grab onto. Oops, a little girl slid unceremoniously down to the bottom with a thud, brushed off the dirt, joined her friend, and off they went.

The bridge was symbolic of life; arched to signify that life's journey is difficult to reach the other world. Plants and flowers did not fill the entire garden, but sprinkled here and there were small trees and a few shrubs indigenous to this valley. This garden was the spirit of the valley but yet also Japanese.

Imprisoned without due process

Ringo-en Garden

"Library of Congress, Prints and Photographs Division, LC-A35-4-M-10."

Imprisoned without due process

In the darkest hour
Heart filled with anxiety
An Angel appears

An Angel Opens the Gate

It was now several months later. I had just completed one year of teaching Physics, attended the first Manzanar High School graduation, and now was preparing for the next year's session. One day, I noticed on the Administration's bulletin board a posting for qualified individuals to teach Conversational Japanese to Army Reservists at the University of Minnesota. My heart beat faster. I read and reread the notice, for this could mean an opportunity to leave Manzanar - freedom beyond the gate. Quickly, I fumbled around for paper and pencil. This could be a dream-come-true. Immediately, I drew up my resume to send to the University of Minnesota inquiring about the language program. Meanwhile, I decided to go to the Manzanar school office and make an appointment to see the Superintendent of Manzanar Schools, Dr. Genevieve Carter, and inform her of my plans and request for a reference from her. For a few weeks I waited for a reply. I kept telling myself, "If I don't get the job, it's ok. I'll manage somehow till another opportunity comes through." But I kept hoping.

Then one day. I received an acceptance letter from the University of Minnesota detailing all of travel arrangements. But suddenly I felt a cold chill. I remembered the Questionnaire 27 and 28 that I had agonized over and over. I had not answer the two questions capriciously. But I realized that my leave now might depend on the answer to those two questions? Would the consequence of my answers to the Loyalty Questionnaire become a roadblock?

I returned to Block 26 to inform *Okaasan* about the possibility of leaving the camp. I waited for Mother to return from her employment at the camp's sewing factory.

"*Okasan, Okaeri nasai* (Mother welcome home)*,"* I greeted her.

Imprisoned without due process

."*Hai, tadaima*, yes I'm here, she replied.

"*Okaasan*, I have the possibility to leave camp to teach *Nihongo*, Japanese Language, at the University of Minnesota, but I am worried about the family for *Otoosan* (Father) is not home," I spoke with great hesitation.

"*Sorewa iikoto desu neh* (that's very good thing, yes it is), mother replied, "*Shimpai wa nai yo* (no need to worry), Kasorikku Huada (Catholic Father) *ni yotte* (according to), '*Otoosan wa sugu karimasu* (Father will return soon)'," she continued. *Koko wa anatano shorai de naiyo* (This place is not your future). *Shipaishinaide,kono ii shugyoukikai ni yukinasi* (Without worrying, go for this good job opportunity), she said with firmness.

With a sigh of relief to hear that *Otoosan* will be back with the family, I decided not to worry Okaasan about my answers to the Loyalty questionnaire. I explained to her what the posting stated and that I would write to the University to apply for the job.

Okaasan said, "You studied Japanese with diligence and did well; I'm sure you will have a good chance for getting the job."

The next day, I hurried to meet with Dr. Genevieve Carter.

Dr Genevieve Carter, who was sent to Manzanar from the University of California to study and report on the impact of the evacuation for the department of sociology in May 1942, had become the Superintendent of the Manzanar schools. Initially there werc no plans for cstablishing schools at Manzanar. The evacuation had of course forced school age children to leave before the end of their school year. There had been no organized programs in the beginning to keep school age children focused and growing up in a normal way. Family, the core of Japanese culture was torn asunder.

The parents, concerned about their children growing up without any direction, pressured the administration to establish a summer program. Dr. Carter found that there were no guidelines for communication between project and evacuees, recruiting teachers, establishing supplies, adequate buildings for education, and housing on the site for the teachers. Dr. Carter was thrust into this chaotic time to set up a school program.

Imprisoned without due process

I first met Dr. Carter when she had announced the recruitment program for teachers among evacuees to augment the credentialed Caucasian staff. I had been impressed with her easy demeanor and sincerity towards education for the children in camp. I had taken an education course from Dr. Carter.

Now, while I fidgeted in my chair, Dr. Carter was calm and engaging that made me feel at ease. She remembered me as one of fourteen individuals of the original two hundred or more applicants who had succeeded in finishing the educational classes. She said she appreciated my effort to make the education program successful. I explained that I had an opportunity to leave Manzanar, a dream that I had had ever since I came to Manzanar. I said, "I am sorry I would have to quit as a teacher if I were to be accepted by the University of Minnesota. Would you write a letter of reference for me?"

Dr. Carter said she would gladly be a reference for me and not to worry about leaving the teaching assignment since the projects primary goal was to encourage evacuees to leave the camp.

I explained further that I had a special circumstance that might not allow me to leave even if I were to be accepted by the University Of Minnesota. "I answered "No, No" on the Loyalty Questionnaire," I told her. I explained my extenuating circumstance about the Family: Mother who could only answer 'No, No,' Father who was imprisoned by the US government but his whereabouts unknown, brother in the US Army, and underage sister. At the time, if I answered "Yes, Yes," our family would be surely torn apart and possibly never see each other again. My answer had not been an easy one and had been a heart-wrenching moment. But time has passed. Now that Mother will no longer be without her husband, I can without hesitation answer what I really believe, "Yes, yes."

Dr. Carter said to me, "Write to the Administration what you have just told me. I am sure they will reconsider your answers. In fact, I am among the review staff and will support you in your request."

Imprisoned without due process

I was relieved and thanked Dr. Genevieve Carter for her time and support.

As mothers always will and always do, dote on their children, she said, "It's very cold where you are going. You will need some warm clothes for your trip." Unfortunately, we were behind barbed wires and there were no department stores, but only a one room canteen and general store. To my surprise, Sears Roebuck had received permission to set up a catalogue service in the canteen. We spent the day leafing through the catalogue for an overcoat, footlocker, and other items for my trip. Mother had to be selective since the internment had impacted the family finances.

My departure was several weeks ahead, and while I waiting, I noticed that *Okaasan* was not present during the evenings. I just thought that she was still busy with her commitment to the Catholic Church since she said they had accepted her into the faith as a sister. One day, just before I was packing my belongings for the trip, mother appeared with several pair's slacks in her arms and said, "These are for your trip." I was surprised and asked mother, "When did you buy these?" "Oh, I bought the material and sewed these pants at the sewing shop. The supervisor said I could use the machine at night to make these." All I could say was, "*Okaasan, arigatoo*, Mother, thank you."

A week before I left, *Otoosan* returned from his imprisonment at the US Federal Prison Santa Fe, New Mexico. I did not see the proud and dedicated man of yesteryear. He was just an empty shell of someone I had once been so proud of. Try as I may, the words simply bounced off of him. He was mute, oblivious to my presence. To say, "*Otoosan, okaerinasi*, Father, welcome home." Home? That would have been an insult to him.

After leaving Manzanar, I never talked much about the experience. Even with my immediate family, words were always hidden deep inside. But several years later, when the camps were gone and I had returned from my job with the University of Minnesota, Dr. Genevieve Carter was the first person I went to see, and we spoke of Manzanar, and I thanked her for her considerate support. Again I found a warm, engaging, and caring person. She was my Angel that opened the gate to freedom.

Dr. Genevieve Carter, Superintendant of Schools

Manzanar Graduation Celebration
Dr. Genevieve Carter, Superintendent of Education to my left

Imprisoned without due process

Stand at the Crossroad
No guarantees on choices
Life's a risk, be brave

Crossroads

After four days and three nights on an old Southern Pacific coach, there I was, at my destination, tired, numb, and grimy from sitting on the hard coach seat. Suddenly, I felt a cold dry sweat across my brow, for I was having second thoughts about this moment. Did I imagine or create my own crossroads a few months ago? Was my decision rash? I had an opportunity to choose: to stay or not stay in camp. However bizarre this thought might be, life in Manzanar was safe. There were no worries about tomorrow, and tomorrow, and tomorrow. I had all the comforts of home: a room, a bed, and three meals a day. However, my freedom was bounded by the barbed wires and watchtower. It was a life in a cocoon, carefree about what might or might not happen. But, who was I? Wasn't it time to come out of my shell?

I chose freedom over a safe haven. There would be unknowns, but I was not alone. When I had told my mother what I wished to do, she did not protest or shed tears. She, in her own way, prepared me for my journey. When it is time to leave, the mother knows and gently nudges her brood from the nest.

This was the last stop for this train. People were gathering their things while ignoring a gum wrapper, crumpled newspaper, half eaten sandwich, and anything that was too much of a bother to deal with in their haste to leave. But of course, I was raised to do. I left my seat as clean as I'd found it, left no trace of my presence, for it was the simple act of respect for others. I waited for a moment while the crowd thinned out, and then moved quickly towards the exit. I followed the passengers to the train station. Inside the building, I found myself in a huge open area where people were either milling around or sitting on rows and rows of oak colored benches. Everything appeared to be made of granite colored marble. The ample lighting within this foyer surprised me since I saw no massive light fixtures. But up towards the ceiling, I saw sunlight shining through the large light wells. "Is this how it feels to be in a mausoleum?" I wondered as I waited for someone from the Methodist Church hostel to greet me.

I had arrived at Minneapolis, Minnesota's Great Northern Station on Hennepin Avenue. I was free once more.

Teaching Conversational Japanese to US Army Reservist at

The University of Minnesota, MN

Imprisoned without due process

Uncommon Yankee Nisei

You're not one of us
How sharp and hollow those words
But I am Bushi

Joseph Kurihara

The angry voice I heard shouting loudly on December 5, 1945, at the fateful gathering of Manzanar Internees near the Manzanar Police Station, was the voice of Joseph Kurihara. I sensed the anger deep inside his soul that burst out. It was a pent up volcano ready to erupt!

But I was focused on the raw recruits fully armed facing the crowd. I was shocked to see a lone soldier squatted on the ground hugging a machine gun fully loaded, cocked, and aimed at the crowd. This was not a place for me to be. Those raw recruits with their M1s looked too trigger happy for my money. We looked like the enemy and this was our fate. It could turn ugly at any moment. I quickly turned and went back to my humble abode.

As I had suspected, a sudden surge by the spectators mistaken as a hostile action was met with gun fire. Two teenage Nisei died from bullet wounds and ten others were injured in that senseless gathering.

Years later, I learned that it was Joseph Y. Kurihara who was shouting at that fateful gathering. He had a right to be angry.

Who was this man who would bear the guilt of the death of two Nisei for the rest of his life?

Joseph Y. Kurihara was born in 1895 in Kaua'i, one of the islands in the Hawaiian Island chain. His father had emigrated from Japan to work on the sugar plantation.

At the age of twenty, departed for San Francisco, where he attended St. Ignatius High School. With the outbreak of the First World War, Kurihara volunteered to serve in the US Army.

Kurihara was one of two million WWI GI's, out of the four million that served in Europe during WWI. He was a member of

Imprisoned without due process

the 85 Division that had trained for eight months and left for the port of embarkation, New York on July 16, 1918. Then on July 30, 1918, The Division left for Liverpool, England. From Liverpool they traveled to Southampton and then boarded ships to France. Units from the Division were sent to replace other troops already there. The rest were sent to De Coetquidan, France to train for day and night maneuvers.

It would be nightmare trip to the front at Toul, France because they were transported on cattle cars with floors saturated with urine and filthy floors. Then from Toul the unit marched for two days and two nights through sticky mud and shared the dugouts with rats. Even the animals pulling the artillery carts were refusing to move through the sticky mud. Worst of all, they had to pass by the stench and maggots feeding on rotting flesh of dead soldiers.

On October 29, 1918, the 128 Field Artillery arrived near the Western Front Line, France. There they could hear the roar of the canon and German canon shells bursting everywhere. Even at night, flares bursting overhead. Death could be eminent that left a sense of despair for not knowing when your time would end.

The unit was preparing for an assault on Metz, Germany, a heavily fortified town and the great canon tht was ceaselessly bombarding their position ceaselessly. It was November 11, 1918 when Armistice was declared .The cost to America, 49,000 killed and 230,000 wounded. But America's loss was dwarfed by the Europeans that had fought the Germans longer.

Kurihara served in Germany until September 1919, and returned to Presidio of San Francisco to be discharged from the army. He was in for a rude awakening...

Still in uniform, when boarded a streetcar, someone called him a Jap and spit at him.

Unlike Hawaii, anti Asian hostility was alive on the West Coast. Then, Congress eventually passed the immigration law prohibiting further immigration of Japanese and barring Asians from owning property and to become citizens.

Imprisoned without due process

But Kurihara, while in the US Army uniform, was not alone to be singled out as Jap in San Francisco, CA...

In 1945, when WW II ended, Inouye, a veteran of the 100/442 Combat Battalion who lost an arm in the Battle of the Gothic Line, boarded a streetcar in San Francisco. To his surprise, a Caucasian called him a Jap and shouted out to him to get off the streetcar. Inouye was a **Medal of Honor** recipient He was also born in Hawaii and later to become a US Senator from Hawaii and served as Senator for 50 years.

The following (From Wikipedia, the free encyclopedia) describes his heroic action on 21 April 1945, in the vicinity of San Terenzo, Italy. While attacking a defended ridge guarding an important road junction, Second Lieutenant Inouye skillfully directed his platoon through a hail of automatic weapons and small arms fire, in a swift enveloping movement that resulted in the capture of an artillery and mortar post and brought his men to within 40 years of the hostile force. Emplaced in bunkers and rock formations, the enemy halted the advance with crossfire from three machineguns. With complete disregard for his personal safety, Second Lieutenant Inouye crawled up the treacherous slope to within five yards of the nearest machine gun and hurled two grenades, destroying the emplacement. Before the enemy could retaliate, he stood up and neutralized a second machine gun nest. Although wounded by sniper's bullet, he continued to engage other hostile positions at close range until an exploding grenade shattered his right arm. Despite the intense pain, he refused evacuation and continued t direct his platoon enemy resistance was broken and his men were again deployed in defensive positions. In the attack 25 enemy soldiers were killed and eight others captured.

Prejudice against Nisei had not died in San Francisco.

. After being honorably discharged, Joseph Kurihara lived in Los Angeles, where he attended Southwestern University, graduating in 1924 with a bachelor's degree in commercial science and a certificate of accountancy. For the next nine years he worked as an accountant, as part-owner and operator of two wholesale produce companies, as an auditor and then manager of a seafood

Imprisoned without due process

packing company, and as a salesman for a company that sold equipment to supermarket. Even with a college degree, he was limited to jobs in farming, fishing, gardening, domestic service, and work related to food distribution. Other areas of employment were largely closed, even to other Nisei university graduates. This was the prejudice and denial of equality imposed on all Nisei that would last for many years since.

Joseph Kurihara was a remarkable generous person of high moral character helping other Japanese deal with discrimination. Compared to other Japanese Americans on the West Coast, he was older than most Nisei. When Japan attacked Pearl Harbor, the average age of the Nisei was 17 years old. At the time, most Japanese families could not own property under California's Alien Land Law that prohibited "aliens ineligible for citizenship" (Chinese and Japanese) from owning property in the state. Thus, Issei who were renting or leasing property could not buy and own the land until their children were of legal age. Remarkably, Kurihara would purchase the property in his name but would relinquish the title when one of the off springs became of legal age. It was a generous and selfless act.

In the mid-1930s, Kurihara turned to his love of the sea. He learned the skill of navigation and found a job as navigator of a Portuguese tuna clipper. He was aboard the "'Belle of Portugal'" when war broke out between the United States and Japan. He was arrested when return to port at San Pedro, CA on December 7, 1941.

After President Franklin Roosevelt issued Executive Order 9066, Kurihara attended a meeting of the Citizens Federation of Southern California to learn about the FDR's directive. There he heard Mike Masaoka, Field Secretary of the Japanese American Citizens League (JACL); tell the audience that he had recently met with Lieutenant General John DeWitt. Masaoka urged compliance with the order to move. Kurihara "felt sick" when he heard this. While the forced removal had angered him, Masaoka's effort to assist the U.S. government in its unjustifiable expulsion of innocent and defenseless people was too much for Kurihara to stomach.

The JACL started a as a social-political group among young Japanese Americans. It should be noted that at the time of December 7, 1941, the average age of young Japanese Americans was approximately 17 years old. It should be also noted that the Issei controlled the affairs of the family and the affairs of the Japanese community. There was a language barrier because the Japanese language it complex and difficult to master. It would take several years until the Issei were financially able to establish a Japanese school. Even when the Kibei return from Japan, they were not included in the affairs of the Japanese Community. Thus, the JACL did not represent all of the Japanese and were never selected to represent them. The JACL to act in behave of all Japanese in America was ludicrous and unwarranted.

I remember too that my brother, who was attending UCLA (1935-1939), started a JACL chapter in Santa Monica. I was among those who were invited to join. We spent several meetings learning about Robert's Rule of Order. It was a good beginning for young Nisei to begin to interact with one another.

Then December 7, 1941 shocked our group to the core.

But worst of all, when my brother learned that the members of the JACL without resolve, meekly capitulated to our US Government wishes, he dissolved the JACL Chapter in Santa Monica.

I too was shocked!

The action words were counter to what I had learned about my rights under our Constitution as a citizen.

Had they forgotten the words of Patrick Henry "Give me liberty or give me death?"

I cancelled my membership immediately.

At the JACL meeting Joseph Kurihara attended, he thought these so-called leaders were "a bunch of spineless Americans." His sentiments were not his alone. He vowed that he would "fight" and "crush" "in whatever camp [he] happened to find them." He would take this determination with him to Manzanar. When all internees

Imprisoned without due process

were required to answer and sign off on the Loyalty Questionnaire, Joseph Kurihara was among the "No, No's" and quickly moved out of Manzanar and sent to Moab jail then to Leupp and then to Tule Lake in December of 1943. He was singled and brutally treated by the guards. There were two distinct camps at Tulelake. One camp housed the normal evacuees. The other was a camp for active protester against the unconstitutional imprisonment. He was imprisoned with the active "No Nos." Later, he renounced his US citizenship under the Renunciation Act of 1944, and among the 316 who did not seek to restore their citizenship after the war's end. He was deported with the first 'Prisoners of War" in 1945.

He worked for the United States Army, Japan as a translator in Sasebo, Nagasaki before moving to Tokyo, where he lived until his death.

Joe Kurihara, age 22, in U.S. Army uniform, 1917.

Courtesy of Grace Fukumoto

Densho ID: Densho

Imprisoned without due process

Men boarding first post-war transport for Nikkei destined for Japan, Seattle, November 1945.
Courtesy National Archives.

Imprisoned without due process

Sadao Munemori.

Sadao Munemori, Yankee Samurai

Sadao Munemori was born on August 17, 1922 to parents who emigrated from Hiroshima, Japan. His father died in 1938. He grew up in Glendale, California and graduated from Lincoln High School in 1940. He worked as an auto mechanic after graduating High School.

While not drafted under the first Selective Service Act of 1940, he enlisted in the army in November of 1941. Sadao was one of those Nisei who were left in limbo in the army because the US Army did not know how to deal with Asian enlistees because he did not fall into the category of draftees. He was a square peg trying to fit in a round hole. He was also sent to the Midwest army base where few or if any Asians were stationed. He would end up for permanent KP duty.

If Sadao Munemori expected to serve in active duty oversea, he would be disappointed because all nations had become isolationists after World War I, the war that was to end all wars. Even though Germany was ravaging Europe and poised to attack Britain, FDR could not declare war to help Britain because Congress had installed a Neutrality Act. Yet, FDR was doing everything possible to help Britain short of sending American troops to England for only Congress could declare war.

Ironically, his army group was assigned to set up the camp at Camp Savage, MN in preparation for the Military Intelligence Service Language School (MISLS) to relocate from Crissy Field, San Francisco, California. Japanese American recruits sent to MISLS were drafted in America's first selective service act of 1940 to learn Japan's Military Language. They were a select group who already were well versed in the Japanese language. The assignment was intensive stressful six month schooling. Sadao returned to Camp Shelby for he was not well versed in the Japanese language.

When Japan attacked Pearl Harbor, FDR declared war and because of a Tri-Party Pac between Germany, Italy, and Japan, FDR could now declare War on Germany and Italy.

Thus, when Japanese American soldiers were allowed to reenter active service in March 1943, Munemori volunteered to be part of the all-*Nisei* **442nd Regimental Combat Team**. This segregated army unit was made up entirely of Japanese Americans, with most initial recruits coming from Hawaii.[10]

The 442 Regimental Combat Team consisted of mainly Hawaiians Japanese Americans and later, Nisei volunteers from internment camps joined the ranks. While they were both Japanese Americans, there was a great difference between the two dissimilar young men that lead to fights. The Hawaiian volunteers were loud and boisterous and spoke Pidgin English (a language that grew out of the workers from several nations who had a hard time communicating not only among themselves but with the brutal plantation bosses) on the Hawaiian plantation. The mainland volunteers were more reserved in their behavior and spoke Standard English. Frequent fights occurred because the Hawaiians felt that the mainland Nisei were putting them down with their Standard English.

The Commander of the Combat Team worried about the friction between the two Japanese American groups decided that he would ask the Hawaiian Nisei to join the Stateside Nisei on the furlough to one of the Relocation Camp in Rohwer, Arkansas.

On the way to the camp, the Hawaiians were singing out loud and strumming their ukuleles. Then a sudden realization came to the Hawaiians when saw the barbwire enclosure with searchlights and guards on watchtowers overlooking the camp ground. The shock of seeing families crowded into hastily built tarpaper covered barracks hit them. Their crime, they looked like the enemy. All animosity drained away for they realized what the Nisei from mainland America was fighting for.

Imprisoned without due process

It was a solemn ride bus ride back to Camp. The 442nd Regimental Combat Team now became one fighting unit with respect for each other. It was now "Go for Broke!"

Munemori was sent overseas in April of 1944 as the 442nd was the replacement unit for the 100th Battalion that incurred great casualties. He saw action in Italy, then in France, where he took part in the rescue of the Lost Battalion. The 442nd consisting about 2,000 men who fought tree to tree in the densely wooded Vosges Mountains located in Northern France near the German border. After days of near constant fighting the 442nd had suffered roughly 1,000 casualties. 200 soldiers were killed in action (or missing) with over 800 seriously wounded, the 442nd rescued 211 Texas Rangers who were surrounded by German troops for many weeks. Other US units tried but turned back from rescuing them because the cost was too great.

At the end of the battle, General Dahlquist asked the 442nd to pass in review. He then asked, "Where are all the men?"

"Sorry sir... this is all we have left" replied a teary-eyed officer.

In 1945, he returned with the 442nd to Italy. In the assault on the Gothic Line on the morning of April 5, he found himself in charge of his squad when his squad leader fell wounded. Trapped with two others in a shell crater by machine gun fire with grenades being hurled at them, Munemori crawled out of the crater and knocked out the enemy machine gun nests with grenades. Scrambling back to the crater, a grenade bounced off his helmet and into the crater. He smothered it with his body and was killed instantly. The other two men suffered concussions and partial deafness but survived. For his heroic actions, Munemori was posthumously awarded the Congressional Medal of Honor, the only one awarded to a Nisei in the immediate aftermath of the war. (A review in the 1990s led to the awarding of twenty additional medals to Japanese American soldiers for their actions in World War II.) The medal was presented to his mother on March 13, 1946.

Imprisoned without due process

In 1948, the 10,000 ton troop ship "Wilson Victory" was renamed the "Pvt. Sadao S. Munemori." In addition, the interchange of the 105 and 405 freeways in Los Angeles is named the "Sadao S. Munemori Memorial Interchange, Medal of Honor World War II" and in 1993, the "Sadao S. Munemori Hall" at the U.S. Army Reserve Complex in West Los Angeles was dedicated. Most recently the town of Pietrasanta, Italy dedicated a statue of Munemori by sculptor Marcello Tommasi on April 25, 2000.
Ben tamashiro 3/15/1985 Hawaii Herald

Authored by Brian Niiya, Densho

In 1925 Roosevelt had written about Japanese immigration: "Californians have properly objected on the sound basic grounds that Japanese immigrants are not capable of assimilation into the American population.

Nobody mentioned that the US Government barred the Issei from owning property and to become citizens. Then FDR vilified them that they could not become assimilated into American mainstream. Remember that the Japanese were recruited to work in place of the Chinese who vilified as the "Yellow Peril."

But then, America had not heard the likes of Sadao Munemori who was the icon of the Bushido spirit and a true patriot.

Imprisoned without due process

Dr. Gordon Sato
Lifetime humanitarian, Eritrea, AF

What is the measure of a man who would after some 40 years seek me out, his former Physics teacher, to thank me for inspiring him to get a college education?

Those were two little words, "Thank you." were humbling words for me to hear from a former student.

Sato, Gordon
San Pedro

He was Gordon Sato a student in my Physics class at Manzanar California, America's concentration camp imprisoning Nikkei during WWII. Gordon went on to tell me tht he was leaving soon to visit Eritrea, Africa. He showed me a document titled "Manzanar Project" and he said that he wanted t help the country out of poverty. At the time, I didn't realize the full impact of his endeavor. Nor did I know about his life after I left Manzanar.

When I left Manzanar, I closed that dark chapter from my mind for fear of stirring up deep feelings of betrayal by my Country. Then in 2011, I read a two line article in the newspaper, "Eritrea, Africa declines further US Foreign Aid."

"Wow, he did achieve it!" flashed through my mind.

Immediately, I guessed that Dr. Gordon Sato had used US Foreign Aid to sponsor his Manzanar Project. I was thoroughly impressed that he had succeeded in helping a beleaguered nation out of poverty and to become self sufficient, I was dead wrong on how he funded his Manzanar Project.

I began to look for Dr. Gordon Sato to congratulate him on achieving his Manzanar Project.

Dr. Gordon Sato had used his own resources and his time to help Eritrea out of its plight. The following is his story.

Sato was born in Los Angeles in 1926. His father was an Issei and his mother was a **Nisei**. He was raised on Terminal Island, East San Pedro where a substantial number of Japanese lived there close to the fishing industry and canneries. However, the area was the home of the US Pacific Fleet. Consequently, the Japanese there were among the first to be relocated. Worse still, prominent members of the community were arrested and sent to jails leaving the family without knowledge of the family affair. There are stories that some had only 24 hours 48 hours to round up their lives and business. The vultures came on the hapless families to steal or cheat them out of the possessions.

In 1942 his family was forced to move to the **Manzanar** relocation camp for internment of Japanese Americans in the Owens Desert of California. He attended Manzanar High School in the camp where he was a member of the camp baseball team and played saxophone in the camp jazz band called the Jive Bombers. During internment in Manzanar he learned the challenges of gardening in a desert, the importance of becoming self-sufficient under deprived conditions, and sympathy toward aggrieved peoples. After graduation from Manzanar High School in 1944, he attended Central College in Pella, Iowa for a year while working at the Wakonda Country Club before enlisting in the US Army and served in Korea.

When Dr. Gordon Sato phoned me and visited me in 1992, he didn't tell me much about his life but he was very enthused as he described briefly about his Manzanar Project and that he was leaving for Eritrea, Africa. I believe, ever since being imprisoned at Manzanar, he wanted something good to come out of that place of injustice. My commitment and dedication to teach Physics must have left a great deep impression on Gordon Sato. I am moved that

Imprisoned without due process

I had inspired him to get a college education that he could now fulfill his dream.

After reading about Eritrea declining further US Foreign Aid., I began to research about Dr. Gordon Sato and his Manzanar Project. His story is a tribute to his greatness and yet one of deep dedication, benevolence, and humility.

Supported by the GI bill, Sato received a bachelor's degree in biochemistry at the **Californian** 1951 and obtained a Ph.D. in biophysics at the **California Institute of Technology** in 1955. He was a professor, researcher at various universities and finally as director of **the W. Alton Jones Cell Science Center, Lake Placid, New York** (1983 to 1992). Sato subsequently resigned as director and devoted himself full-time to the Manzanar Project.

Sato is co-inventor with his son, **Denry** Sato, and John **Mendelson,** CEO of **The University of Texas M. D. Anderson Cancer Center,** of the original technology used in chemotherapeutic agents based on inhibiting the epidermal as Cetuximab (Erbitux).

Dr. Gordon Sato is a recipient of a number f awards and honors: Laureate, Rolex Award, 2002; Blue Planet Award, 2005; Lewis S. **Rosenstiel** Award, 1981; in 1984 he was elected to the National Academy of Sciences for his contributions to cell biology.

I was able to contact Dr. Gordon Sato to congratulate him on his great accomplishment. Subsequently, he sent me this book, "Manzanar Tree." I contacted one of the authors, Susan L. Roth and sent her this comment:

Imprisoned without due process

A few years ago, Dr. Gordon Sato sent me a copy of your book, "Mangrove Tree" and I would like to share with you the Gordon Sato that I know. I too was imprisoned at Manzanar because I looked like the enemy. I took 24 units of UC educational courses to qualify as Provisional High School teacher at Manzanar. I was selected to teach high school Physics. Gordon Sato was a student in my Physics class. It was some forty years after Manzanar closed that Gordon Sato phoned me and said he wanted to come and see me. He told me that he had received as BS degree from USC 1951 and his Doctorate degree from Caltech in 1955. He said he was ready to go to Eritrea, Africa on scientific project to help Eritrea out of poverty. He said he called The Manzanar Project and handed me a copy of that project. I did not know of all of the scientific research he had done nor the scientific accomplishment he had achieved. While this Nisei who has dedicated his Gordon Sato.

For a student to seek his former teacher is in itself a wonderful tribute to me. But then, at our meeting, Gordon Sato said he wanted to thank me for inspiring him to get a college education. Two little words, "Thank You" showed me a man who stands tall among all of us with courage and humility. I too had hoped that something good would come out of that place of injustice. Little did I know that I had planted a seed that would blossom into something beautiful for the world to see. That is the Gordon Sato that I know.

Tadashi Kishi

We love this reminder that behind every leader, innovator, scientist, and world changer, there's a great teacher! Thank you, Gordon Sato, and thank you Tadashi Kishi!

By Susan L. Roth and Cindy Trumbore:

Imprisoned without due process

Over 2 million mangrove trees

Imprisoned without due process

The rest of the story

As the well known radio announcer, Paul Harvey said, "The Rest of the story."

When WWII ended, my contract was terminated at the end of the school semester. I decided to return to Los Angeles, CA to try to reenter UCLA to complete my college education.

Just as I step into my parents' house, my mother handed me an envelope and said, "There is an important letter from the Government."

It was a draft notice!

Subsequently, I was drafted and sent to Fort Lewis Washington for Basic Training, There were a number Nisei who were also drafted. After three months of Basic Training, all of the Japanese Americans were singled out and sent to Presidio of Monterey to learn Military Japanese under the Military Intelligent Service (MIS).

Imprisoned without due process

After six months of schooling, we were sent over sea and attached to General MacArthur's GHQ in Tokyo, Occupied Japan. We were assigned as interpreters or translators.

One group had the boring task of translating wartime documents. I was assigned to the British Legation as interpreter investigating war crimes in the South Pacific.

One day, I passed my baptism of fire as an interpreter for an Australian Officer. At the time, the British Officer was trying to interrogate an ex-Japanese soldier. His ATIS/MIS interpreter was a heavyset Nisei. I looked at the flushed face of the Australian officer because he was having a hard time understanding, not with the ex-soldier but with the Nisei interpreter.

Imprisoned without due process

"My bloody arse. I can't understand a bloody word my interpreter was saying!" blurted out the officer.

He saw me sitting, waved his hand at me and said, "Will you take his place!"

Apparently the officer couldn't understand his interpreter's Pidgin English.

The Nisei, whose place I was taking, must have come from the rural area of Hawaii where Pidgin English was the standard dialect. He got up and left quickly as I took over his place.

The Australian officer looked directly at me and said in a heavy Australian accent, "Ask the ex-Japanese soldier, 'was the captured British soldier in *"Jaw-ile?"*'"

For a second, the word *"Jaw-ile"* threw me for a loop until I realized he meant "jail."

I did "jolly good" on that one. Then the next one came.

"Was the man a *"Nah e vee"* man? I again hesitated for second. Then it dawned on me tht he meant "Navy."

I breezed through the rest of the interrogation after passing the first line of fire.

The third group of Nisei was interpreters questioning ex-prisoners of war imprisoned and now released by Russia. The aim was to determine if the prisoners could provide war time information on Russia's military installations and, most important, any information about Russian atomic effort and atomic facilities.

In September 1948, I returned to San Francisco, CA to enter UC Berkeley to continue my college education. I received my BA in Physics in 1949 and MS in Math in 1951.

I worked briefly at McDonald Douglas Aircraft, Long Beach, CA; a year at Los Alamos National Laboratory, Los Alamos, NM, and transferred to Lawrence Livermore National Laboratory from January 3, 1953 to January30, 1989.

Imprisoned without due process

In 2011, President Obama presented the Congressional Gold Medals to members of the 100/442 Battalion and the Military Intelligent Service during WWII. I am a recipient of that Congressional Gold Medal for my service to our Country during WW II as member of ATIS/MIS Military Intelligence Service.

....

Imprisoned without due process

Freedom, Liberty
It's in our Constitution
With Justice for all

Epilogue

Many decades have past ever since I closed the gate of Manzanar behind me. Meanwhile, our Government that had surreptitiously changed my classification from 1 A to 4 C, enemy alien – a convenient justification to intern me at Manzanar as an alien - restored my status and back to 1 A, citizen, because the US Army desperately needed individuals with the knowledge of Japanese language. Strange but true, they sent me to the MIS school at Presidio of Monterey to learn Military Japanese so that I could serve oversea in occupied Japan. I was a member of the Military Intelligence Service/Allied Interpreter and Translation Section (MIS/ATIS) attached to General Macarthur's GHQ in Tokyo, Japan. I saw the devastation that we had inflicted on wood and paper houses with napalm bombs. I learned of the suffering and atrocities in the South Pacific while serving as interpreter for the British Legation investigating war crimes. I stood on ground zero at Nagasaki, Japan and paused for a moment as I saw the grotesque form of structures bent and melted by the tremendous energy released by "Fat Man," the second atomic bomb. I set foot on Iwo Jima, an island that was void of vegetation and saw Mount Suribachi that was won at a great cost of human lives. I set foot on Guam, king pin of America's defense in the Pacific, that was lost and won again. I stood on the shores of Kwajalein in the Marshall Islands. Gone were the palm trees that waved gently in the breeze. Silent were the sound of guns, the cry of wounded and dying soldiers, and the roar incessant bombings by our Air Force. I stood on the beach and watched the waves lap the shoreline. I thought for a moment that if my parents didn't have the courage to immigrate to America, I could have been one of those Japanese soldiers killed on this desolate lonely island. It was a sobering thought. But it was Hickam Field when I deplaned that I reflected silently at the horrific attack by Japan on a Sunday morning, for that moment had turned my life upside down.

Although the Emperor of Japan had declared unconditional surrender to the allied forces, his act did not end the hatred that was spawned by our President Franklin Delano Roosevelt on all Japanese whether citizen or alien. In contrast, on July 15, 1945, surviving members of the Japanese American 442/100 Regimental Combat Team marched down Constitutional Avenue in Washington, DC and stood at attention on the White House lawn as President Truman presented them with the seventh presidential citation. He addressed them and said, "You have fought for the free nations of the world ... You have fought not only the enemy, you fought prejudice, and you have won." How hollow those words sounded to me when I tried to realize the American Dream in the small cowboy town of Livermore, California.

One day, my son came running home because a classmate in his elementary school had called him names, chased him, threw a rock at him, and injured him. That night, I sat with my sons and talked about what had happened. They were both aware that my wife and I had been imprisoned at internment camps, Poston, Arizona and Manzanar, California, respectively. I told them that I would not tolerate them to treat anyone poorly because they were different. Over the years I have observed their conduct and I am proud that they have both live exemplary lives of tolerance and compassion.

August 10, 1988, President Ronald Reagan signed into law the Civil Liberties Act of 1988 granting each surviving internee $20,000 in compensation, with payments beginning in 1990. The legislation stated that government actions were based on "race prejudice, war hysteria, and a failure of political leadership" as opposed to genuine legitimacy. Then on November 21, 1989, President George H. W. Bush signed into law HR 2991, which established entitlement status for redress funding and a formal apology.

Imprisoned without due process

When the check came in the mail, my wife and I held the check and looked at each other. For a moment nothing was said. Yet in that brief silence, we both remembered what our parents had gone through, struggled to survive under extreme prejudice, only to lose everything. But they were gone. Without hesitation, we both said, "This belongs to our parents and not us. Let's send the checks to our sons as gifts to remember our parents."

Imprisoned without due process

Apology

THE WHITE HOUSE
WASHINGTON

A monetary sum and words alone cannot restore lost years or erase painful memories; neither can they fully convey our Nation's resolve to rectify injustice and to uphold the rights of individuals. We can never fully right the wrongs of the past. But we can take a clear stand for justice and recognize that serious injustices were done to Japanese Americans during World War II.

In enacting a law calling for restitution and offering a sincere apology, your fellow Americans have, in a very real sense, renewed their traditional commitment to the ideals of freedom, equality, and justice. You and your family have our best wishes for the future.

Sincerely,

GEORGE BUSH
PRESIDENT OF THE UNITED STATES

OCTOBER 1990

Apology 1990

Imprisoned without due process

Be aware our Constitution caught a virus!

But the story does not end here for the tale of three individuals from Manzanar need to be remembered.

They are: Joseph Kurihara, a veteran of WWI, imprisoned at Manzanar in spite of the fact that he had already proven his loyalty to the United State. He was a man of principle, honesty of his convictions, finally driven to renounce his citizenship and leave for Japan in protest of his rights a citizen being denied.

Sadao Munemori, who volunteered to serve even before the US Selective Service Act of 1940 was enacted by President Franklin D. Roosevelt. His family was also imprisoned at Manzanar. He was a member of the 100/442 Regimental Battalion and for his bravery, he was awarded posthumously the Medal of Honor.

Dr. Gordon Sato, who was a student in my Physics class at Manzanar, CA, has dedicated his life to humanitarian efforts because he wanted something good to come out of that place of injustice. He has saved Eritrea, AF, one of the poorest nation in Africa out poverty and to become self sufficient. He uses his own resources from professorship, research and from heading various scientific efforts and not US Foreign Aid Funds. And to this day, he continues his humanitarian and scientific efforts.

But the story of injustice may not end here for we live in a dangerous world. In 2011, following President George W. Bush, President Barrack Obama has signed into law under the National Defense Act of 2011 that anyone can be arrested, imprisoned without due process for an unspecified amount of time.

Yes, your rights as citizen can be in jeopardy.

Imprisoned without due process

Protect you from harm

But

Not your rights or freedom

Bibliography

Densho Encyclopedia, Nisei war hero, Sadao Munemori

Eileen H. Tamura: *In Defense of Justice*, University of Illinois Press, 2013.

The Hawaii Herald, March 15, 1985, The Hawaii Nisei Story, The Congressional Medal of Honor, Sadao Munemori

Susan L. Roth & Cindy Trumbore, *The Mangrove Tree*, Lee & Low Books Inc. New York

Unran, Harlan D. Manzanar: Historic Study/Special History Study, *The Evacuation and Relocation of Persons of Japanese Ancestry During World War II: A Historic study of the Manzanar Relocation Center*, United State Department of the Interior National Park Service, 1996

Williams, Carey. *Prejudice: Japanese Americans Symbol of Racial Intolerance*, Little, Brown and Company, Boston, MA, 1945.

Imprisoned without due process

The Author

Tadashi Kishi, a Nisei (second generation Japanese American) was born in Culver City, California, December 11, 1921. He spent most of his childhood in Santa Monica, California and graduated from Samohi, Santa Monica High School in 1939. He was attending UCLA majoring in Physics when the war broke out. After President Roosevelt issued Executive Order 9066, he was uprooted and interned at Manzanar, California with other Japanese in the Santa Monica area.

While interned at Manzanar, he took 24 units of Educational courses at night under the University of California's Extension School in order to qualify to teach high school Physics at the Manzanar High School. After teaching one year of Physics, he applied to teach Conversational Japanese at the University of Minnesota as an opportunity to seek freedom from internment.

Later, he was inducted in the US Army, trained in Military Japanese at the Presidio of Monterey, California, and served in Occupied Japan as a soldier and interpreter for MIS/ATIS assigned to General Macarthur's GHQ.

After his discharge from the Army, he continued his college education at UC Berkeley and graduated with a MA degree in Math. He began his career at the Los Alamos Scientific Laboratory (LASL) and transferred to the Lawrence Livermore National Laboratory (LLNL) at Livermore, California. He was a Math/Programmer, System designer, and supervisor for large scale scientific computers: IBM 700 series, LARC, and CDC 6600. He was the project manager for the LLNL's commitment to utilize the ARPA ILLIAC IV for scientific application. He returned from the ARPA assignment and was a staff member of the Computation Department investigating special system for large scale scientific applications. His last assignment was the Division Leader for programmers and technicians for scientific applications, small computer systems for the Magnetic Fusion Test Facility (MFTF), and the Laser Project.

Imprisoned without due process

He has written several technical papers, given seminars at .universities and won the best technical paper at the IEEE Computer Conference in San Francisco, California.

He is also a recipient of the Congressional Gold Medal for the service to our Country during WWII.

The story, Ringo-en came from the third chapter of the author's memoir, "Lady on the Bridge," a story that reveals who his mother was and her struggles to survive in a hostile land. The book has been approved by the Nikkei Writers Guild and is currently waiting to be published.

Imprisoned is a follow up on Ringo-en about three Nisei who have left a historical mark on the "Imprisonment of Nikkei at Manzanar."

www.ingramcontent.com/pod-product-compliance
Lightning Source LLC
Chambersburg PA
CBHW070213290526
45789CB00002B/984